"Eden Boudreau's debut memoir is a searing and unflinching record of the assault and aftermath of sexual violence. Admirers of Alice Sebold and Sarah Polley should make room on their shelf for this evocative account of rape by a third partner within a polyamorous marriage—and the internal and systemic wounds which occur as a result. With her incisive wit, heartbreaking insight, and riveting storytelling, Boudreau has earned my admiration as both a talented writer and a steadfast survivor."

—Amber Cowie, author of *Last One Alive*

"*Crying Wolf* is a phoenix rising from the ash of Boudreau's pain. In her stunning and eloquent debut, Boudreau takes readers on a harrowing journey through some of her darkest days, while holding a mirror to a society that perpetuates the shaming of those who live in the margins. Readers will close *Crying Wolf* with a sense of having been changed by the story of healing and returning to oneself, but most of all, will find themselves hopeful for the future."

—Kelly S. Thompson, national bestselling author of *Girls Need Not Apply* and *Still, I Cannot Save You*

Crying Wolf

A Memoir

Eden Boudreau

Book*hug Press
Toronto 2023

Library and Archives Canada Cataloguing in Publication
Title: Crying wolf / Eden Boudreau.
Names: Boudreau, Eden, author.
Identifiers: Canadiana (print) 20220458006 | Canadiana (ebook) 20220458057
ISBN 9781771668088 (softcover)
ISBN 9781771668101 (PDF)
ISBN 9781771668095 (EPUB)
Subjects: LCSH: Boudreau, Eden. | LCSH: Rape victims—Canada—Biography. | LCGFT: Autobiographies.
Classification: LCC HV6569.C3 B68 2023 | DDC 362.88392092—dc23

The production of this book was made possible through the generous assistance of the Canada Council for the Arts and the Ontario Arts Council. Book*hug Press also acknowledges the support of the Government of Canada through the Canada Book Fund and the Government of Ontario through the Ontario Book Publishing Tax Credit and the Ontario Book Fund.

Book*hug Press acknowledges that the land on which we operate is the traditional territory of many nations, including the Mississaugas of the Credit, the Anishnabeg, the Chippewa, the Haudenosaunee, and the Wendat peoples. We recognize the enduring presence of many diverse First Nations, Inuit, and Métis peoples and are grateful for the opportunity to meet and work on this territory.

For the little girl who lost her voice somewhere along the way.
And for the woman, who found it again.
Louder and unwavering this time.

Author's Note

Thank you. Thank you for finding this book. For opening its pages and giving it a chance to tell you my story. Because it's not just my story. It may be yours as well. Or your mother's, sister's, husband's, brother's, or best friend's. Maybe you can't actually relate to the trauma of sexual violence, but you are choosing to educate yourself on what one in three women experience every day in North America. Either way, thank you.

The events depicted in the following pages, which took place between the fall of 2017 and the summer of 2019, are presented as I remember them, and through my own perspective. I think it's important to note this because, often, people remember things differently. Even those closest to you may have different recollections, or may be hurt by your truth, or try to contest it. That does not invalidate it or make it unreliable. Remember this.

Choosing to write about my early life, marriage, polyamorous partners, and recovery from sexual assault was my decision, and not the decision of those who were present during those times. In an effort to respect their privacy, certain names of people and places, and/or identifying traits have been changed.

I also think it's important to note that the experiences you'll read here are those of a cis-gendered white woman living in a country with access to publicly funded healthcare. There is no competition when it comes to who has experienced worse trauma. Yes, my non-monogamy, bisexuality, and kink-forward lifestyle puts me outside the realm of traditional living. But it would be ignorant to whitewash this experience and not acknowledge that those in marginalized communities have, and continue to endure, this kind of violence, lack of support, and injustice at appallingly higher rates.

All this is to say that there is a problem. Women, those who identify as female, and all those in vulnerable situations deserve to live without fear. There needs to be change. Reading, educating, and speaking out, as I am about to do in this book, are some of the best places to start.

Thank you again, and never stop trusting the power of sharing your story.

—Eden Boudreau

Contents

CHAPTER I

Cat and Mouse

CAPTURING A FISTFUL OF MY HAIR IN HIS GRIP, HIS FINGERNAILS clawed against the soft skin of my nape. Blood had begun to crust in fine lines where my lips had split when he had gnawed on them, over and over, ignoring my pleas to stop. Wrenching my head back toward him, away from the freedom of the open car door, he held me there and studied my pained expression. It was almost as if he wanted to linger in the moment a little longer, before the aroma of my terror could escape into the night air.

This wasn't consensual submissive-versus-dominant roleplay. It wasn't the willful relinquishing of power and control that often took months to arrive at with a trusted partner. It was neither fetish nor kink, not even playful teasing. It was something altogether wrong, regardless of where you fell on the vanilla scale in the bedroom.

Positioning my ear against his mouth, voice still thick with greed, he whispered, "You belong to me now. You know that, right?"

Squeezing my eyes shut, I willed myself not to tremble under his touch again. Using the only strength I had left, I nodded.

In the thirty-seven years that I've been alive, I have been raped—twice.

The first time was when I was seventeen and unconscious after too much sour apple vodka and too little supervision. The second was on this muggy September night, just beyond the city lights of Toronto. By a man that even my husband, Joe, had given the green light to. A man we'd both naively assumed might be a potential new partner after what should have been a casual first encounter.

And in that moment, my nails digging into the leather car seat as I tried not to fall into his grasp again, I thought that maybe if I hadn't ignored the obvious red flags or the sick sensation of intuition in my gut from the moment we met, it would have been. Casual. Unremarkable. Just another night.

Regrettably, shoulda-coulda-wouldas have never worked in a woman's favour, and that night was no different.

* * *

The first thing that occurred to me when I'd arrived at Jack's, a busy sports bar on the corner of Yonge and some forgotten side street just north of the city, was how it stood out. The place was an ugly, towering block of cement and neon lights, flanked by rows of small, fragrant Korean takeout's, bustling laundromats, and quiet townhouses.

It had been a year since Joe and I decided to take our three sons and as many belongings as we could pack in a twenty-six-foot moving truck and relocate from Halifax to a quiet suburb in the Greater Toronto Area. The electric nightlife of King Street West, the endless euphoria of consumerism in Dundas Square, the tight-lipped elegance of Yorkville—none of it had ever interested me that much. What did, however, was the opportunity.

Ontario—Toronto, specifically—was a place with endless opportunities, especially for two determined self-starters like myself and Joe. We had spent too many years working endless hours to increase someone else's profit margin while barely being able to put food on the table for ourselves.

So, when we were presented with the chance for Joe to start his own business if we relocated, it was a no-brainer. But times like these—as I waded through the sea of mandatory-date-night couples and hyped-up newly single twentysomethings with the bass of an unintelligible rap song throbbing against the side of my head—reminded me that Toronto still didn't feel like home.

Finding two open stools along the long chrome bar top, I scooted up onto one and plopped my bag on the other. I'd always enjoyed sitting at the bar, even if my short legs swung like a toddler in a highchair; it gave me a chance to people-watch. This was possibly my favourite activity.

Perched happily on a stool, I'd construct little stories in my mind about the people nearby, imagining great love affairs or shady acquisitions. Sometimes I'd take out a notebook and pretend I was Sylvia Plath. I'd write down the stories, promising myself that at some point down the road I would turn them into something bigger. It was, unfortunately, a promise that was almost always forgotten when there were laundry and lunches and play dates needing my attention.

Either way, it always kept me busy when I was on a solo night out or waiting for a date, like tonight. Just a week before, I'd been mindlessly scrolling through a dating app, this one catering to polyamorous people like myself and Joe, when a man caught my attention. Liam was a thirty-three-year-old IT manager for a bank by day and an amateur boxer by night. Tall, with broad shoulders and a narrow waist, eyes the colour of root beer. Skin that looked as if it might feel like velvet if I were to touch it. And, best of all, he'd liked me first, opening with an equal parts charming and intriguing string of messages until I finally liked him back and replied.

It didn't take long for his attention to send me swooning. Call it astrological predisposition—I'm a Scorpio, after all. Or maybe it was still being relatively fresh to the non-monogamy lifestyle, two years at that point, and a baby bisexual who'd so far had zero luck with the ladies. Either way, I was happy to get asked out for some conversation and drinks.

Except I wouldn't actually be drinking. One of my firm rules when meeting someone on a first date was that I drove myself there and home. It made it easier to say goodbye and split whenever I felt the night starting to drag. And, bonus, it also allowed me to avoid the uncomfortable passenger-seat groping when he'd undoubtedly ask how I planned to "pay him back" for the drive home. Every woman has been there or known someone who has, so I figured it was best to just avoid that scene altogether.

"Here's your Coke." The bartender slid a glass toward me, the ice clinking against the sides. "I put a little straw in there for you." He took my bill and winked as he dug in his cash box to make change. Leaving a few coins on the bar for him, I nodded my thanks. The straw trick was something my older sister, Kami, had taught me during one of her sober stints. When non-sober friends saw you sipping your drink through a straw, they would assume you were partaking in the festivities and be less likely to turn on the peer pressure. It worked for first dates as well.

As I took my first sip, a heavy hand seized my shoulder and I jumped in my seat. Mortified, I clamped a hand over my mouth as an embarrassing squeak escaped my lips.

"Hey there, gorgeous." Liam snaked in beside me and leaned against the bar. He was taller than I thought, well over six feet, and heavier too. Bulky muscles swelled beneath his blue and heather-grey button-down shirt. What had appeared impressive in his profile felt a lot more imposing now that he was towering over me.

"Hey." I patted the top of his hand and nudged it gently from my shoulder, motioning to the open seat beside me. "I was just going to text to say I got us a couple spots at the bar. Do you want me to wave over the server?"

Conscious that Liam's eyes had not once diverted from their mission to explore every visible part of my body, I tugged the hem of my T-shirt down over the waistband of my jeans.

"Nah." Abruptly, he turned and started for a set of stairs that led to the second floor. He called over his shoulder as I fumbled with my purse and drink in an effort to catch up, "Let's go upstairs where we can have more privacy."

I stopped at the bottom of the stairs. Words of protest perched on my lips, but before I could use them, he reached out and grabbed my hand. Not palm-to-palm or fingers softly interlaced, but an awkward snatching and pulling, the way a mother might yank a screaming toddler from the chaos of a grocery line.

The upper floor was quieter with booths lining the back wall and another smaller bar at the top of the stairs. Leading me to a booth in the farthest corner, Liam snapped at a passing server and waved for her to follow us. When he finally released his grip on my hand, I took the opportunity to slide into the side of the booth, staying close enough to the edge that there wouldn't be enough room for him to slide in beside me.

I could feel the tiny hairs on the back of my neck stand up every time he glanced over at me, letting his eyes linger on my body a little too long. If I'd been starring in a movie, this is exactly when the deafening warning sirens and alarms would have started to blare directly over my head.

* * *

But this wasn't a movie. It wasn't a piece of fiction in which a feisty young woman can throw her drink in the face of any man that makes her uncomfortable. This was the real world, where women are ambushed on jogging paths in broad daylight, or mowed down in crowds by incels with a bad case of blue balls, or worse. This was the world where women are labelled hysterical, dramatic, and over-sensitive when they dare to push back even the slightest against the patriarchal society that has raised them to associate modesty and obedience with safety.

It was also the world where women have become desensitized to the wandering gazes of men. At least I had. It started when I was twelve, and my dirty blond hair and speckled green eyes gave me that *Sweet Valley High*-girl vibe that grown men in their twenties apparently found appealing. And it continued as I progressed into adulthood, even after my body had softened from growing and carrying three tiny humans. The colourful patchwork of ink on my skin was the perfect excuse for them to stop and stare, occasionally brazen enough to let a hand roam as well.

And when that happened, I'd respond like the good girls we've all been raised to be. Instead of slapping their hand away, I would politely laugh and make myself as small as possible. I wouldn't make waves. After all, not making waves was the underlying message of the "rules" that are shared with every young girl at some point in her early life in order to help her stay safe when dating. Funny enough, this information is usually imparted well before we stop believing boys have cooties, never mind consider going on dates. Some of those rules were:

1. First dates should always be during the day or early evening, when it's still light out, and always in public.
2. Don't drink too much, but don't be a bummer either.
3. Tell someone where you're going and when you should be back.
4. Dress cute, but not too revealing.
5. Flirt, but don't lead them on.
6. And, in the event that something bad happens, remember not to bother yelling "help." Yell "fire," or no one will come.

To me, these unofficial rules of girlhood always seemed to deliver an odd message: *We're damned if we do and damned if we don't, so take all the precautions anyway.* Unfortunately, the people doling out these rules failed to consider that sometimes the predator they were designed to protect us against knew them as well. And knew exactly how to get around them.

* * *

"What are you drinking?" Liam nodded toward my still-full glass while the server waited to take his order. I thought about telling him I wasn't drinking because I had to drive. Seemed like a legitimate reason. But before I could even attempt the truth, his attention was back on ordering. "Just bring her a double rum and Coke." He paused. "Diet. And I'll take a vodka soda. Make that a double too."

Again, I thought about declining. Thanking him but insisting on sticking with sobriety. Then I remembered the rules: *Don't be rude. And definitely don't make him mad.* So, when the drinks arrived and I could smell the heavy pour of rum before he'd even passed mine to me, I ignored those hairs standing up on the back of my neck and did what I'd been taught to do. I politely tucked it beside my unfinished Coke and pretended to be intrigued as Liam dominated the conversation.

While Liam was significantly more imposing in person than I'd anticipated, he was just as charismatic. Only now, that charisma had an irritating vein of arrogance in it, and that had me fidgeting in my seat and checking the time on my phone.

"…This kid had no idea what he was getting into. Took one hook to the jaw and I laid him out flat. They told me later that, apparently, I'd broken it in three places," Liam proudly recalled. He'd been rambling on about the last time he'd stepped into the ring as an amateur boxer, a bullet point from his dating profile that he enjoyed bringing up, repeatedly.

"Umm oh wow, that sounds like a crazy fight." I checked my phone again, willing Joe to interrupt with some random parenting emergency that would give me an excuse to leave early.

Leaning across the table, Liam nudged the phone from my grip, slid it over to the side of the table, and scooped up my hand, squeezing my fingers just a little too tight. "Stop worrying about your phone." He nodded toward my collection of glasses. "Finish your drink."

It didn't feel like a suggestion.

"You know what…" I slowly pulled my hand from his grip, flexing my fingers until the feeling returned. "I've had a wicked upset stomach all day and rum always makes it worse, so I'll probably just keep nursing it. But, thank you."

I pushed aside the half-empty Coke and cradled the full rum mix between my palms, hoping it would appease him and maybe avoid another bone-grinding hand hold. Before I could pretend to still be enjoying myself, Liam snatched the drink away, tipped it back to his lips, and swallowed it in one loud gulp. Slamming the glass back down on the tabletop, loud enough to draw attention from our server, he sat and stared at my face for an uncomfortable length of time. Then, as if he were flicking a light switch, he turned on his charming smile and returned to his monologue.

My skin exploded in goosebumps, and not the good kind.

For the next hour, I feigned interest, trying to come up with an exit strategy that would end the night with the least amount of drama. After Liam had returned from one of his many bathroom visits, I made a lame excuse about the babysitter needing to leave early and the kids' dad being away for work, giving me no option but to head home. As he watched me with a confused and disappointed stare, I gathered my purse and stood to leave.

More agile than I'd expected, Liam bounced out of his seat and stood in the way of my exit. "Why don't you let me drive you home? That way we have more time to get to know each other better." He raised a dark brow and smirked as he reached for his coat.

"Oh, that's okay. I actually drove here on my own." I edged around him, careful not to make it too apparent I was about to bolt.

I could see his body stiffen, a sourness seeping into his voice. "Well, at least let me give you a lift to your car."

Slowly heading toward the stairs, I raised a hand up between us. "No, no. Don't be silly. I'm just in one of the lots behind the bar. The streetlights will get me there." I quickened my pace until I reached the top of the stairs. As I started down them, I called over my shoulder, "Thanks again, it was nice to meet you. 'Night!"

When I'd arrived earlier that evening, the parking lot directly behind the bar had been full, so I'd opted for the building's second lot. Both lots were fenced in on three sides by rickety wood railings; the only distinction between the four rows of parking spots in each were heavily worn tread marks in the dirt. It had been relatively empty before I'd gone in, but now the rows of cars and trucks were tightly packed, creating a metal maze with the only light to guide you pooled in the far corner under one flickering streetlight. It seemed a little more eerie now than it had before, but being outside, without the confinement of walls and one-sided conversations, took some of the edge off.

As I was weaving my way through the cars in the first lot—only two rows, a hop over the fence into the second lot, a scuttle to avoid the puddle, and one more row of cars until I made it to mine—my phone buzzed in the bottom of my purse. I stopped and rummaged for it in the dark. Pulling it out, I tapped the screen, bringing it to life and seeing a text message from Joe:

9/26/17
JOE: *Heading to bed now babe, love you. Have fun and get home safe.*

I couldn't help but smile. There was a time not so long ago when I'd genuinely thought our relationship was over, that we'd never find a way to make it work, but we had. With a lot—*a lot*—of trial and error, we'd eventually landed somewhere outside the bounds of a traditional marriage and were now happier than we'd ever been. It was a feeling I never wanted to lose.

A familiar and unwanted voice interrupted my thoughts: "A pretty girl like yourself shouldn't be walking in the dark alone." A hand grabbed at my arm, squeezing too tight. I looked up to see Liam. He had followed me out to the parking lot. "Come on, at least let me drive you to your car."

I twisted out of his grip. "That's nice of you, but really, I'm parked right over there. Goodnight." I started moving more quickly in the direction of my car. A knot in my stomach the size of a softball threw off my balance. I cursed myself for not just taking the sidewalk past the first lot and making my way into the second through the gate. It wasn't as if that route would have been significantly safer, but it was a few feet closer to the string of homes that lined the opposite side of the street. From there, maybe someone would hear me if I yelled. But instead, I had let my guard down, and recovering from that mistake wasn't going to be easy.

Liam was quicker and apparently more adept at playing cat-and-mouse than I was. He continued to call after me, protesting that I shouldn't be walking alone. And when I paused for a second too long before climbing over the wooden railing, he grabbed my upper arm, pinching the flesh under his fingertips, and pulled me against his side.

"I'll be insulted if you don't let me be a gentleman," he insisted as he turned me around and pushed me in the opposite direction of my car. I stumbled over my words, trying to form my own protest as we moved between a large SUV and a black four-door Mercedes. With one hand still in control of my arm, he used his other hand to pop open the passenger-side door of the Mercedes and shove me into the seat. Before he could slam my feet in the door, I pulled them in and hugged my bag to my chest. My breath started to come in heavy pants and the intrusive thoughts in my mind began to battle each other.

What should I do? Don't make him mad. Should I get out and run? You're overreacting. Will anyone hear me if I scream from inside the car? Not if he shuts you up first. Just sit quietly and keep your hands to yourself. Thank him and get out as soon as you can.

In that moment, the internal dialogue was mine, but it also belonged to all of the women who had been in this position before me. My older sister Kami, my mother, grandmother, aunts, cousins, co-workers, and friends. It was the generational wisdom passed down to every little girl when boys are being taught to climb trees.

When those boys are choosing their college courses, and we're being taught how to hold our keys between our knuckles. When they are being taught how to succeed, and we're being taught how to survive.

Two Roads Diverged

A MOMENT AFTER LIAM SLAMMED THE PASSENGER CAR DOOR, HE hopped into the driver's side and turned the car on. It purred to life and we sat in silence while he absentmindedly fiddled with the heater knobs. I could tell he was waiting to make his move. A hand on the knee. A caress of my arm. A flirtatious word or two whispered in my ear. I had been here before with men I had zero interest in fooling around with, and yet needed a ride home from our failed date. This was exactly what I'd been trying to avoid by driving myself.

Distracted as I contemplated ways to politely turn him down, again, without insulting his masculinity, I wasn't prepared for what came next. One second, Liam was in his seat; the next, he was on top of me.

* * *

In hindsight, I'm aware that it took an incredible amount of agility for a man more than six feet tall to climb over the centre console, pull the lever beside my seat to recline it, slamming my body backward, and then settle his entire weight on top of me while aggressively smashing his mouth into mine. This was not his first time. He had done this before.

"Stop." My words muffled against his lips. "No."

He nipped my lip, so I said it louder. "Stop! I don't want to do this. I'm sorry but I don't want to do this."

It was too late. I'd fallen right into his trap. With one hand around my neck and the other blindly fumbling with the button of my jeans, he hissed in my ear, "You wanted this, I could tell. You've been eye-fucking me all night."

I turned my head away from his hot, wet breath and tried to shimmy upward on the seat and out of his grip. But all that ended up doing was creating a space between my waist and his, just big enough for him to shove his whole hand down the front of my pants and underwear. His rough fingers immediately entered me. I winced at the abrasive touch.

My continued pleas to stop were ignored as Liam raised up slightly, removing his hand from inside me and shoving my pants down farther, the denim scraping against my skin. His left hand was still around my throat, the tension only slightly lessened. His eyes burned into mine. I dared to stare back.

"Tell me you like it," he growled.

A dizzying wave of resentment and anger rushed over me. It was one thing to try to take what had not been given to him freely, but his insistence that I enjoy it exhausted my last reserves of patience and politeness.

Slowly, deliberately, I pushed up against his hand and said, "No."

That was when the world went black.

I'm not sure how many times he punched me. Probably only once or twice. But that was all it took to splinter my vision and knock me unconscious for long enough that when I came to, he had removed my pants and ripped off my underwear.

Eventually the stars faded from my vision and I could focus clearly again—only now I wished for the opposite.

Above me, his massive body lurched as he ground his limp penis against my pelvic bone. Over and over, he demanded I tell him I liked it, and with every refusal, silent or spoken, he would grab my chin, squeeze my jaw, and wrench it to face him. He tried to kiss my pinched lips, gnawing at them and shoving his tongue into my mouth. I wasn't playing along and neither was his dick; it was still limp against me, and I could tell it was pissing him off. That was when he went from simply playing with his dinner to ripping it apart.

Balling his hand into a tight fist, he attempted to shove it inside me. When I felt the thin skin between my legs tearing, I couldn't help but cry out in pain. That's when I witnessed the one moment that will never be erased from my memory: Liam's face lit up with pleasure.

Now I knew what he really wanted—to cause pain. Every time I flinched or whimpered or sucked in a sharp breath, I could feel him growing hard against my leg. A venomous smirk painted his face as he pumped his fist in and out of me, my pain fuelling his sick lust.

For what felt like an eternity but was likely only an hour, Liam switched between penetrating me with his penis and his hands. When that alone wasn't giving him enough motivation to stay erect, he would twist and bite my nipples, hard enough to leave bright pink rings of teeth impressions in my pale flesh. He would pinch my ass, slap me across the face, or choke me with both hands, squeezing until darkness crept in around the edges of my vision. Part of me worried it would never end; another part wanted to end it all.

At some point, he managed to stay hard long enough to continually thrust into me like a jackhammer. Finally finding his rhythm, he moaned and panted in between spitting degrading filth in my face.

"Yeah, you like that don't you, little whore. I knew when I saw you you'd be a great fuck. Take it like a bitch."

Turning away from the pin pricks of his words, I focused instead on the night sky stretched above us just outside the car window. I willed my mind to remove itself from my body by thinking of anything other than what was happening to me, anything other than this moment.

My thoughts escaped to my home, in the suburbs north of Toronto. It wasn't the rural coastal life Joe and I were used to, but it was quiet, the people were friendly, and, most importantly, it was where my family waited for me.

I thought of my three sons. Milo, the youngest who was the human personification of a golden retriever—all happiness and energy. Cassius, who preferred to go by Cash, was in the middle, and the spitting image of his father with his scattered freckles and almond-shaped blue eyes. Then there was Declyn, the oldest, who had come from a relationship previous to my marriage with Joe—already so long and lanky we were positive he would tower over us all sooner rather than later. I hoped they were snuggled into their beds, fast asleep. Not a worry in the world. Never ever considering that I might not return home to them. And yet, that exact fear screamed inside the walls of my mind.

What if the pain isn't enough? What if his pleasure can't peak until he's taken more than my body—until he's taken my life?

Cringing under his last painful pump, I was pulled from my thoughts and back to the present as Liam groaned and collapsed on top of me with a grunt. I froze, unsure if this was simply an interlude or if he had exhausted his greed. Slowly, so slowly, I placed the palms of my hands on his chest. His panting had slowed and I worried that he had fallen asleep on top of me. I pushed up softly against the full weight of his body. The small sensation must have jogged him from his euphoria nap. Abruptly, he forced himself off of me and back over the centre console, landing in his seat before pulling his pants up.

"Well, that was fun." He glanced over at me and smirked. "You're a little freak." He snickered as if he'd caught me in a lie, as if I'd been playing the coy, shy girl but he had managed to pull the kinky out of me. I couldn't tell if it was an act or if he genuinely thought that this had all been some sick roleplay. Maybe he was hoping it would spur me to place blame on my own behaviours that night. Or maybe he thought all he had to do was will my unspoken consent into actuality and it would void any wrongdoing. More than likely, it was just another well-calculated tactic to keep me quiet.

Painfully, I pulled my pants back on. My skin crawled with what felt like a thousand biting ants. An uncontrollable shaking started in my teeth, then moved down my shoulders to my arms, hands, and legs. I searched the dark footwell of the car for my bag and cell phone, while Liam rambled on about how much fun he'd had and that we should do it again soon. Finally finding my belongings and writing my underwear off as a loss, I was reaching for the door handle when I heard the loud click of automatic locks.

"When?" he growled. I stared at him, not understanding. He leaned closer. "When are we doing this again?"

My mouth was dry, tinged with the taste of pennies from repeatedly biting my tongue to keep myself from crying. It caused me to stammer. "I'm not really sure... really busy week coming up with the kids and work and stuff... probably won't be able to lock anything in but maybe in a few weeks..." I inched closer to the door as I rambled, my mind on escape.

Liam narrowed his eyes as he watched me, seemingly deciding whether he liked my answer or not.

"You're not going to tell your husband about this right?" He paused. "You're not going to tell anyone, right?" I shook my head back and forth. "Good." He sat back and smiled. "'Cause it's really easy to find people."

The threat wasn't so much thinly veiled as a punch to the gut. I nodded and held his stare, willing him to just let me out.

The moment I heard the click of the locks releasing, my hand pulled on the handle and I pushed the door open. I looked out at the dirt lot below my feet and let the wash of cool night air ground me, just enough to propel me into motion. But as I leaned away, ready to move when my feet hit the ground, his thick fingers grabbed a chunk of my hair and pulled me back in by the nape of my neck.

I yelped, letting go of the door and fumbling to untwine his hand from my hair. Pain cut through my scalp as he tightened his grip, wrenching my head backward. He leaned close to my ear and whispered, "You belong to me now. You know that, right?"

Without hesitation I nodded. I would have agreed to anything just to be freed from his grasp. Satisfied, Liam released me, and I stumbled out of the car and onto my feet. They felt new, unsure of how to operate. Slamming the car door behind me, I walked as fast as I could through the lot, over the fence, and to my car. I was afraid if I ran my feet would fail me.

Frantically hitting the unlock button on my key fob, I slipped into the driver's seat and punched the button again to lock the doors. Waiting until I saw his lights turn on and the sleek black Mercedes pull away, I squeezed the steering wheel so tightly my knuckles tingled.

When I was sure he wasn't going to circle back and follow me, I threw the car into drive and fled from the lot as fast as I could. At first, I took a zig-zagging path east before finally heading north on the back streets. After a little while, I came to an intersection. I could keep heading straight toward the highway that would take me home. Or I could turn back, find the nearest police station, and ask to speak with an officer.

I looked out through the windshield into the night and whispered to myself, "Two roads diverged in a yellow wood…"

The line was from one of the most frequently quoted poems in history. Written in 1916, Robert Frost's *The Road Not Taken* is a staple for tired high school teachers trying to impart wisdom about forging your own path as opposed to sticking to the mainstream. It was a verse that I'd often repeat to myself when I had a difficult choice in front of me.

This choice, however, was not one I could ever have predicted, because I had not chosen to arrive at this bend in the road. Someone else's actions had forced me this way, leaving me without a compass in the aftermath. Whether I wanted to or not, I was taking the path less travelled.

Suddenly, I felt trapped within the walls of my car. My breath started coming in shallow, shaking gulps and hot tears blurred my vision. Pulling the car off the road, I shoved the gear shift into park.

I knew a panic attack was coming. They had been a common occurrence since I was nine years old. Over the years, I'd trained myself to reason my way out of them. I would determine the source of my anxiety—real or a figment of my imagination—and then break it down into manageable chunks. Either it wasn't really as bad as I'd blown it up to be or there were easy solutions, if only I put my mind to it.

But this was different. There was no rationalizing what had happened, no exaggeration of the events. I had just been raped.

Reaching for my phone—I'd tossed it onto the passenger seat when I'd jumped into the car—I swiped across the screen and searched for my sister's phone number. The line rang and rang and rang. Kami still lived on the East Coast near our parents, and they were an hour ahead of us, which meant she was likely asleep. At that moment though, I really needed my big sister.

The phone continued to ring until her voicemail clicked on and I ended the call. I dialled another number; Joe's phone didn't even bother to ring. It must have died after he'd gone to bed. He had a bad habit of losing charging cords, forgetting to find a new one, and letting his battery run out. I cursed myself for not being home to remind him to plug it in.

Wiping away tears with the palms of my hands, I attempted to slow my breathing. In through the nose and out through the mouth. Tapping the phone screen one more time, I dialled three numbers—911. My thumb hovered over the green call button.

There was no reason I shouldn't call the police; I knew this. Their job was literally to serve and protect. But as I sat in the dark on the side of the road, I couldn't help but wonder who they would protect in this particular situation.

Would it be the grown woman whose skin was saturated in ink, who was a "young" mother by today's standards, and who had willingly gone on a date with a man who wasn't her husband? Or would it be the misunderstood gentleman who had clearly been led on and tricked into believing his date was up for a good time, just to have her unfairly persecute him without solid proof?

Anyone with an internet browser or who has picked up a newspaper in the last century knows the answer to that question. Liam was a man with primal instincts; he couldn't be held responsible for what he'd done in the heat of the moment. But because I had chosen to explore my sexuality, with and without my husband, by opening our marriage, educating myself on sex positivity and the kink community, and engaging in respectful intimate relationships with men and women, I was clearly a whore. And I had a sinking feeling that even those who'd taken an oath to protect the innocent would assume the positions of judge and jury long before I'd see the inside of a courtroom.

When I finally made it home—I had to stop three more times to catch my breath—I sprinted from the car to our front door in the darkness. Swinging it open, I accidentally slammed it into the wall while scrambling to close and lock it behind me. I realized too late that my exaggerated entrance must have sounded like a freight train coming through the front window. A half-asleep Joe came running into the front entryway in just his boxers, sleep still creasing his face.

"What the hell, Eden?" He came closer. "Are you okay?"

I didn't know how to answer him. Collapsing into his arms, sobs making it impossible to choke out any words even if I could have found them, my whole body just wanted to sink to the floor. Joe propped me up under one arm and gently tipped my chin up; his eyes searched my face for answers.

"Did you have an accident?" He glanced out the window at the car sitting in the driveway with no obvious dents. I shook my head and laid against his bare chest, the stubble of his chest hair scratching against my cheek. A pregnant pause grew between us and I could feel his arms tighten around me as he started to piece things together.

"Did he hurt you?"

I didn't have to reply; he could tell by the way my body went rigid against his. Before he could probe any further, I pulled away from his chest and looked up at him.

"Please, I need a shower." His blue eyes, somehow still bright in the dim light of the hall, looked so pained. "I just need to be clean."

Joe may not have known exactly what happened, but he knew me. He knew how much I prided myself on being strong under pressure. A show of vulnerability this overt meant I was hurting, badly.

Gently, Joe guided me into the bathroom, keeping a close eye as I shuffled uncomfortably, now that the pain between my legs was blooming. Leaving me to lean against the sink, he leaned over and turned on the taps.

"What can I do?" he asked without looking up, his fingers skimming the water to test the temperature.

"Nothing, there's nothing you can do." I had the feeling he meant more than bring me a Tylenol or find my warm pyjamas. Joe had struggled with his own fair share of adversity growing up, the difference being that what he couldn't solve with his wit and charm he was taught to solve with his fists. That was normal for young men—as normal as it was for young women to be taught to only speak when spoken to. Unfortunately, rushing out into the night to hunt down the man who had harmed his love only made sense in movies. And right now, I needed him here more than anywhere else.

Nodding, Joe kissed me on the forehead. Then, carefully, with just the tips of his fingers, he helped me to undress. I could tell he was avoiding looking at the bruises beginning to form on my skin, but it felt as if he was avoiding looking at me entirely. Another strand of tangled thoughts unspooled.

Is he disappointed in me? Does he think I'm dirty, or tarnished in some way now? Will he ever look at me the same way again?

Not wanting to be naked and seen for any longer than necessary, I wrapped a soft towel around myself. Holding the shower curtain open for me, Joe gently supported my back as I stepped in. I could tell he was being careful not to touch my skin. I knew he was just being sensitive to how raw I clearly was in that moment, but the gesture pricked at my nerves, lending credence to the worries swirling in my mind. Once the hot water hit my face though, all thoughts evaporated.

I was pretty sure Joe had left the bathroom when I realized the only sound I could hear was that of the water pelting my skin and drumming on the bottom of the tub. Reaching down, I cranked the knob all the way to the right and watched as the steam crawled up the sides of the shower tile and out over the curtain. Grabbing a bar of soap, I scrubbed until my skin felt raw. I still felt dirty. So I scrubbed again.

When my flesh was pink and tender, I put down the soap. Then something caught my eye. A ribbon of red snaked down my legs and into the water pooled at my feet. It was coming from where I couldn't see. My head swam with nausea and I sank to the bottom of the tub. I squeezed my eyes shut as the shower pelted my face. I could feel the water beading on my lashes and streaming off my chin. Opening my mouth, I gasped at the hot humid air. It felt like I would never be able to breathe again. Then I heard the door open.

Joe came and sat on the tiny stool we left outside the tub for bath time. I could hear him fidgeting. Reaching up, I shut off the water, the steam and silence boxing us in.

"Seriously, what do I do?" It was a simple question, and it made me love him even more.

I reached out, my hand still dripping wet, and waited until I felt his warm, callused fingers thread through mine. "This all I need right now. This helps."

We sat like that for some time before I asked Joe to help me climb out of the tub and into the loosest clothes we could find. To be honest, I didn't really want anything touching my body, but I also couldn't stand the idea of being naked. Too exposed, too vulnerable.

I did not sleep that night, not even for a brief time. Instead, I lay there in the dark, listening to the sound of my own breathing, making sure I was still alive, because everything in my body and in my mind was telling me the opposite. Telling me I had just died, and that whatever came next would be an entirely different life.

CHAPTER 3

Tea and Consent

THE NEXT MORNING, WITHOUT WAKING JOE, I SLIPPED OUT OF OUR bed and wandered to the living room. Standing in a small pool of sunlight slanting through the blinds, I closed my eyes and soaked it in. Every inch of my body hurt, and yet, at the same time, somehow felt completely numb. It was as if my mind was trying to disassociate itself from the biting pain between my legs.

Blinking against the bright light when I dared to open my eyes, I turned away and spotted my mud-crusted running shoes, discarded by the front door after my last run. At one time I would have been up and out the door, my feet hitting the pavement and drowning out any negativity. In fact, the last 5 a.m. run I'd done was the day before; I realized it might have been the last one for a while.

Buzzing from the kitchen pulled me from my thoughts and I retrieved my cell phone from the counter where Joe had plugged it in to charge last night. I had emailed my manager not long after I'd returned home to let them know there was no way I'd be able to make it in for my shift at Hatha, the hot yoga studio where I'd picked up a part-time gig working the front desk shortly after we had arrived in Ontario.

Back in Halifax, I had spent nearly a decade busting my ass working sixty hours a week as a hair and makeup artist. Both Joe and I had put in the time and energy to grow our careers, and, most importantly, to support our family. But it wasn't what I had dreamed of when I was young. I had wanted to be a writer.

There had been various versions of that dream throughout my life. Growing up in the 90s, when everyone else my age was reading The Baby-Sitters Club and the Goosebumps series, I was engrossed in dystopian tales like *The Giver* and *The Handmaid's Tale*. At first, they were just a way to escape the chaos at home, but eventually they became a conduit to worlds where you could speak truths without being silenced.

Eventually my dreams became loftier and more cinematic. I'd fantasize about catching a plane to New York and using the city as my muse, becoming a serious storyteller in the process. Most people would have gone the higher-education route, learned the basics, and then made the dive into novel writing, but financially, university wasn't an option. Figuring I could work at a trade while chasing my story-writing goals, I went to college for my cosmetology licence. And then the universe threw me a curve ball. In 2004, three months before graduating and just a few weeks after buying a plane ticket to NYC, two little pink lines showed up on a pregnancy test and my whole life changed direction.

Did I think that direction would involve answering phones and filling our student memberships for my local yoga studio? Not likely.

Replying to my manager's email, I lied and blamed my absence on a serious case of stomach flu. Placing my phone back on the charger, I poured myself a cup of coffee from the pot we had programmed to brew every morning. For Joe, caffeine was a necessity when it came to getting through long days of giving orders on jobs sites, but for me it was more than just a stimulant.

Coffee held a strange comfort, being one of the few things my mother and I had bonded over when I was younger. Right around the time I turned eight, she called me into the kitchen of our country duplex one morning and taught me how to make a pot. Fill the carafe with water. Pour it into the back of the machine. Put the filter in the tray. Three scoops of ground coffee. Wait for it to brew.

Growing up, I tended to fall into the shadows. There was a lot of chaotic energy in our house, and it often felt easier to be invisible than to stir up more trouble. My parents had divorced when I was one and Kami was seven. For me, living with just my mother and sister was how it had always been, but Kami had lost my father, even though he dedicated himself to being there every day in some way.

I may have resembled our mother the most, but Kami and my mom were identical in other ways. They both wore their hearts on the sleeves. My father was the stoic, silent one. I gravitated to this because it seemed like less energy to be around and, even as a child, I was tired of fighting. So, I would do anything I could to smooth things over. Which often resulted in acts of service.

For the next eight years, I would bring my mother her coffee almost every morning. She would let me sit at the end of her bed and watch cartoons on the small tube TV while she drank her coffee and did crosswords. It was how I imagined other families spent time together. But as the years went by, more often than not the coffee would go cold on her bedside table. She would sleep long past noon, sometimes still in bed with the covers pulled up tight well after I got home from school. I didn't know then that depression had set in. So I kept bringing her the coffee, eventually making my own and sipping it at the foot of her bed while she slept.

I knew there were other kids who had it worse, the ones who had to hide bruises or went hungry for days. But for a child to grow up too early, to see the frailty of their parents before they've lost their own innocence—this was not what I wanted for my own sons.

Stirring from down the hall drew my attention. Quietly shuffling across the wood floors, I snuck into the younger boys' room to find them thankfully still asleep in their beds. Every new parent remembers the well-meaning but unsolicited advice given to them in the first years of their children's lives. My mother and aunts had been no different, insisting I let the boys sleep in their bassinets or cribs as babies, but I could never bring myself to let them sleep all alone. I would wake up extra early every morning and scoop up the little bundles, taking them back into bed with me and holding them close for as long as I could.

Softly I tiptoed across the room and laid beside Milo, brushing the sandy blond hair off his forehead. Neither of my sons with Joe had inherited their father's bright red hair. That hair was one of the first things that had caught my eye when I met him. Growing up with straight mousey blond hair (that my mother regularly kept in a short mushroom cut), I was always envious when I saw others with vibrant copper or chocolatey brown, like my sister's. And I was still curious as to whether the boys would have traces of their father's ginger roots in their beards someday.

Cash yawned and rolled over in his bed on the opposite side of the room, his shoulder-length hair falling over his pillow in a fan. He was your quintessential middle child. The rebel, the artist, the gentle giant of the family. Where our oldest, Declyn, was patient and a natural caretaker like myself, Cash was quick to action and impulsive like his father.

I wrapped my arms tighter around Milo and squeezed him just a little bit, thinking about how all three boys were on their way to becoming such individual and brilliant humans. Thinking of my sons, still so small and soft, with the faces of grown men pulled me under a wave of sadness like an unseen current. If even one thing had gone differently the night before, I could have easily lost my chance to see all those little moments that were so often taken for granted. My sons could have been dancing alone at their weddings. Their children might never have known their grandmother. Their lives could have been ruined before they'd really even begun. I'd almost fucked it all up.

And so, while I laid there and watched them sleep, I made them a promise. That I would never be so selfish again. Never take chances, even if they were for my contentment, that could negatively impact their lives. They would never have to take care of me because of choices I made. And I would give them the childhood I didn't have. I would do whatever I had to get better. To be a present and happy parent.

As my heart raced in my chest at the mere thought of what I had to do, I worried that keeping my promise might not be so easy. Until then, I would just have to fake it.

* * *

Later that day, we asked a neighbour who worked at the kids' school as a substitute teacher if she'd be willing to watch the boys for a few hours while Joe drove me to a doctor's appointment. We made it sound like a routine check-up. Assured them we'd be back as soon as possible. Put on a smile and waved goodbye as we pulled away from our house. Going through the motions was harder than I'd imagined.

Forty-five minutes later—after battling traffic and wavering between wanting to get checked out and wanting desperately to just go back home—I found myself in the bustling waiting area of the emergency room at Mackenzie Health Hospital. I don't really know what I'd been thinking I was about to walk into. Maybe a clinic with soft, muted tones on the walls, paintings of wildflowers, and overstuffed sofas? Gentle and patient staff. A paper cup filled with warm coffee to sooth my nerves. But whatever I'd imagined was the exact opposite of what greeted me when I walked through those doors.

I'd shuffled into the bewildering chaos of close to fifty other people sandwiched into a muggy waiting room. Growing up as a rough-and-tumble tomboy and then raising three sons, I had been in my fair share of emergency rooms. But this wasn't going to be an in-and-out situation, so after taking a number and sitting in one of the stiff plastic chairs, I sent Joe a text letting him know to head home to be with the kids. I would take a cab back once I was done.

9/27/17
JOE: Absolutely not, I will wait for you. Shoot me a message when you're done. I'm not leaving you.

I breathed a small sigh of relief before inhaling more of the stagnant hospital air.

Not long after I'd shuffled in, a loud voice called my number. When I rose to see who it belonged to, I came face-to-face with a barely-over-twenty-five male nurse who already appeared to have the same jaded demeanor I'd witnessed from time to time in our family doctor. The nurse led me into a cubicle nearby, leaving the door wide open. Other nurses casually passed through to borrow blood pressure cuffs or thermometers.

"Health card?" Without so much as a glance in my direction, the nurse began tapping on the keyboard as he opened a new file on his computer screen. I fumbled to pull the card from my wallet and silently slid it across the table. Either he was completely unaware of how I was shrinking in on myself with every minute that passed or he was actively ignoring it. After inputting my information into the computer, he finally turned to face me, his fingers still poised over the keyboard.

"What brings you in today?"

I couldn't bring myself to answer.

As I glanced from the door back to his impatient eyes, I realized I had two choices. Tell him why I was there, honestly. Or run as fast as I could to who knows where as long as I never had to vocalize what happened. Although the latter was far more appealing, it wouldn't help the pain between my legs that had started throbbing again since I'd arrived at the hospital.

"I was raped last night."

Neither of us moved. The commotion of the emergency waiting room continued to rage all around us while we sat staring at each other for an uncomfortably long time. Then, as if his training had finally returned to the driver's seat, he swivelled back to his computer and frantically tapped on the keys. There were no more questions as he printed off a few sheets from my intake, threw them into a manilla file folder, and herded me down a narrow hallway. He gestured to the row of seats and told me to wait for the nurse.

This area was smaller and pungent with the scent of antibacterial cleaner. I tucked my feet up on the seat of my chair and pulled my knees to my chest. Not an easy posture as a grown woman with the curves that come with age, but it felt comforting to be smaller and less noticeable. But I didn't go unnoticed.

Being in such close proximity to those who have time on their hands, and likely low battery power on their phones, means eyes begin to wander. In particular, the eyes of a young man who sat across from me, shackles on his feet and wrists. A bored-looking police officer hovered at the man's side, oblivious to the way his eyes were following every twitch or fidget of my body. Part of my old self wanted to push back and not waver under the weight of his attention.

As a child I'd been opinionated, but had generally stood on the sidelines. As a youth I desperately tried to find my way without making too many waves. By the time I was fourteen, I'd already earned myself the moniker of the "little pit bull." More bark than bite most of the time. It was Kami who gave me the title. We had never had the traditional big sister-little sister dynamic. When most people met us, they assumed I was the older one. It wasn't a maturity thing so much as behavioural. She was sensitive and I was stubborn. She was the life of the party and I was the one who shut it down.

More times than I could count—times when I ought to have been in my flannel pyjamas at some sleepover or typical teen hangout—I found myself instead standing at the feet of average men, who felt like giants. Who were desperate to let their hands roam and take from Kami whatever they could. I was the child, begging my big sister to come home and somehow making sure she ended up safe in her own bed, spending the rest of the night sitting on the floor beside her to make sure she woke up the next day.

If that girl had been in that hospital hallway, she would have straightened her back and stood her ground. But one by one, small, innocuous similarities between the man across the hall and my attacker began to draw my attention. Even as he sat hunched in his seat, I could tell he was around the same height, with broad shoulders and chest. His hands, though smaller, clenched in a way that made the flesh on his knuckles turn white. He'd hit a woman before, as I'd assumed my attacker also had from the accuracy of his strikes, and I could tell he was thinking of doing it again. It was more than this weak, trembling version of myself could handle.

I finally looked away, only daring to give him one last glance when I heard him chuckle. He'd won his silent game of chicken, and I was yet again the loser. The smirk that smeared across his lips sent a wave of disgust over me. If I had been in a Sunday morning cartoon, my whole face would have shifted to a sickly green.

"Boudreau, Eden?"

A nurse with short brown hair, brushed aggressively to the side, waited with my chart in one hand and the other hand planted firmly on her hip. She didn't even bother to scan the faces of the waiting patients, just tapped her foot on the faded linoleum tiles and stared straight ahead. For a brief moment, I thought about not answering. Letting her grow annoyed and move on to the next patient, and then sneaking out and hurrying back to the safety of my bed. I was already drowning under a tide of emotions just being there; the last thing I wanted to lump on top was the kind of guilt that came from burdening someone who clearly had no time for my shit. It was a feeling that, as a child, I'd grown to know all too well.

But as she called my name a second time, her voice an octave higher with irritation, the instinct to appease was too strong to deny. Hurriedly, as if I hadn't heard her the first time, I stood and silently followed her down a maze of hallways until we hit a dead end. A semicircle nurses' station took up one end of the hall; two doors stood on opposite sides, and a collection of gurneys and IV stands littered the general area. As she shoved a gurney out of the way with her round hip, she muttered a curse under her breath and unlocked the door. I couldn't tell which was the bigger inconvenience, me or the gurney.

The exam room was small, set up like most doctors' offices and painted in that soothing tone I'd been hoping for when I arrived. The space was surprisingly calming. Except for one thing. As I slid onto the examination table, I was startled by the clank of a rather heavy deadbolt being secured on the door and the piercing jingle of the keys as the nurse turned them in the doorknob as well.

She must have noticed how it had spooked me, because for the first time since we'd met in the hall, her tone softened. "For your peace of mind, dear." She patted my knee and took a seat, opening my chart and going over its contents.

"Sweetheart?" Her tone, even though it had softened a little, still had a snap to it.

"Yes, sorry." I shook my head, trying to clear the encroaching fear.

"It's okay." She touched my knee again, clearly aware it was one of the few reassuring gestures that wouldn't make my skin crawl. "I was just saying, I'm Nurse Jane, and I will do your preliminary exam today before the doctor joins us."

I felt stupid, but I had to ask: "It's a woman, right? The doctor?"

Tilting her head to the side and smiling, the way you would when a child asks if the tooth fairy is real, she replied, "Yes, hon, she'll join us shortly." She scribbled a short notation in my file, closed it, and let it teeter on her lap while she leaned closer. "Okay, let's start at the beginning."

I started from when he climbed on top of me in the car. I knew this wasn't exactly the beginning, but it was the sharpest memory I had. Recalling that moment was like seeing a photograph in a vivid rainbow of colours and textures, while everything before it and after I raced to my car was subdued and muted. I made sure to speak calmly and clearly about how I'd said no. How I'd repeated it and how he'd answered with his fists. How he used intimidation and pain to make me aware of the far worse things he could do if I didn't behave and let him take what he wanted. I even found the words to re-live how badly he wanted me to act like I wanted it. But when I had to describe the violation, the penetration with his hands and dick, what he left inside me, it was like fighting a monster of emotion desperate to break down the door and devour me. Somehow I was able to hold it back just long enough to finish with rushing home and my husband helping me into the shower.

I took a shuddering breath, balancing on the edge of a full-blown breakdown. The memories had been on a constant, sickening loop since the moment Liam had released me from his car. But speaking them out loud took away even the most remote possibility it had all been a nightmare. A fictionalized horror I had concocted in my mind. My head rocked on my neck and it was all I could do to keep it upright. Lowering it into my hands, I closed my eyes.

"So this man... wasn't your husband?" Nurse Jane leaned back, her hand travelling to rest on the walkie-talkie clipped to the waist of her scrubs. Immediately, I knew what she was insinuating. We'd all heard the story before: wife cheats, and when her husband finds out, she pretends it wasn't consensual. At least this was the narrative many men had used in defence of their actions. I couldn't imagine any woman who would rather label herself a rape victim than an adulterer.

"I wasn't cheating on my husband." I sat up and swivelled toward her, begging for her full attention. "I wasn't cheating. I know it sounds like it, but I wasn't. This was a date. My husband and I have a different arrangement. Not arrangement... that sounds bad." I balled my hands up and tried a different approach. "We are polyamorous. It's a form of non-monogamy, like an open marriage, but not really. It's not just about sex; it's more than that." I was rambling again, and I worried that I was losing her. I didn't know much, but I knew I desperately wanted her on my team. We stared at each other in silence for an uncomfortable amount of time.

Slowly, Nurse Jane nodded and opened my file. Flipping through the pages, she commented without looking up, "You know, some people in that community, I've been told they have these sort of pre-arranged agreements, you know? And maybe some-times wires get crossed, or miscommunicated." Finally meeting my eyes, she bobbed her head as if encouraging me to remember some imaginary consent agreement that never was.

I shook my head slowly, trying to stop the anger from bubbling to the surface. I wouldn't say I have a short temper; I simply don't have patience for ignorance. As a child, this had led to endless arguments with my mother over my "attitude." I was never cheerful enough or appeasing, always with an opinion and never a filter. Though he never said it, I was sure this made my father endlessly proud. He and my mother were polar opposites. Where she spilled emotions over every situation, he refused to cry even after learning of the passing of his own father. As an adult, I realized neither of these were healthy coping mechanisms, and undoubtedly both had contributed to their messy divorce. As a child though, having not grown up with my father living in my household, I would do anything I could to impress him. Including starting an argument. It had become my specialty.

Now—slowly, clearly enunciating each word so that I would not be seen as yet another hysterical woman—I responded to Nurse Jane. "We are not swingers. We are not part of the fetish commun-ity. We are a non-monogamous married couple who are open to romantic and physical partners in addition to our own relationship." She nodded. Setting aside my chart, she moved to the counter and started removing items from a box with "RAPE KIT" stamped in bright red letters on its top. Seeing those words sent a jolt of panic through my chest. I continued, "And even if we were, which we are not, that doesn't mean consent is always automatically assumed."

I was staring at the back of her faded blue scrubs, willing her to turn around and acknowledge me, to believe me. The fact that I had to work so hard to convince another woman that my marital lifestyle shouldn't factor into my believability, especially a woman who had presumably dedicated her life to helping victims heal, felt like the spark before an explosion.

"Have you ever heard of that tea and consent video? You know, the one where they explain that even if someone invites you over for tea, and you accept, and even if they ask once you've arrived if you still want tea, and you say you do, and even if they pour you a steaming hot cup of tea"—I took a deep breath, my voice shaking—"you still don't have to drink the fucken tea!"

Her shoulders sank. Removing her gloves, she turned toward me. My whole body was shaking now, uncontrollably, like the last leaf on a tree in autumn. She placed both hands on my shoulders and squeezed.

"I'm sorry, I'm so sorry." The tears broke their dam now, rolling down my cheeks to drip off my chin into my lap.

"It's okay." Her voice had lost all its bite. It was barely a whisper over my sobbing. "It'll be okay."

She placed a neatly folded johnny gown in my lap and asked me to change into it while she went to retrieve the doctor. As she left, the deadbolt clicked again, this time from the outside.

I removed my clothes and slid on the thin fabric gown, struggling to knot the ties behind me. I lay back on the table and desperately tried to let my mind wander away from the waves of shame, guilt, and embarrassment. On the wall beside me was a plastic rack filled with pamphlets. On one there was a woman standing on a beach, looking out at the ocean.

When we were young, Kami and I would spend at least two weeks every summer on the Northumberland Shore in New Brunswick at our family's cottage. It was designated time with our father, but for me, it was yet another chance to escape. The ocean was one of the few places I always felt free. You would think, growing up in a province surrounded by water, that you could go into it anytime you like. But the beaches at the cottage had a different feel. You could run through the waves, skip from sandbar to sandbar, and sit around the bonfires until the embers burned out without ever having to worry that when you returned home, there would be another argument, raised voices, more sadness.

So that's what I would do. Hide away on the beach behind the tall strands of wispy grass while wearing socks of sand and seaweed, generally with my little notebooks in tow. I went everywhere with a journal or a book back then. The ocean gave me solace, but the stories kept me company.

I was always a lonely kid. Even when surrounded by people. It made me wonder if even a small portion of my reason for agreeing to an open marriage was the possibility that it might cure that loneliness. Just because I actively avoided attention didn't mean I didn't want it. It was one of those martyr moments that are almost impossible to explain but make sense to those who know them as well.

The turn of the lock brought my attention back to the little room, and I nervously crossed and uncrossed my legs as the doctor entered, followed by Nurse Jane. The doctor was a short, petite woman. Her scrubs were rumpled and her fine brown hair was pulled back tightly off her face. There was no hand-holding or hair-petting with her. Putting on a fresh pair of gloves, she immediately went to work. Barking notations at the nurse, she started from the top.

"Hair missing from the nape, scalp red and inflamed. Bruising under the left eye, and around the neck. Bite marks on left nipple, minor lacerations." She paused, turning my forearms over and looking closer. "Beautiful ink." It was a fleeting moment of connection between me and this woman who was about to become very personal with my very private area.

She maneuvered my feet into the stirrups for the pelvic exam. "Six millimetre tear on the perineum," the doctor mumbled through her mask to Nurse Jane. She met my eyes over the thin paper sheet draped across my thighs. "I can put a stitch in it, if you'd like. It'll be sore for a few days either way." I nodded for her to go ahead. I'd had more than one stitch down there after Milo's birth, and I didn't see the point in turning it down now.

I concentrated on the ceiling tiles as she numbed the area, the sharp prick of the needle making me wince. A low buzzing caught my attention. Nurse Jane removed her glove and glanced at her phone as she pulled it from the pocket of her scrubs. Whispering into the doctor's ear, she anxiously apologized and excused herself. Again the click of the lock echoed in the small room.

A few minutes later, the doctor patted my knees, the universal sign every woman knows to mean that the exam is done. I shimmied up the bed to sit, awkwardly covering my lap with the paper sheet. We sat together in silence as she jotted hasty notes into the kit. When she'd finished, she handed me three prescription slips: a prophylaxis in case I had been exposed to HIV, Plan B in case of pregnancy, and morphine for the pain.

"Oh," she turned back to her pad and quickly scribbled another note. "Here is one for a sleep aid. There are three refills. You don't have to fill it anytime soon, but there will most likely be a time when you'll need it." She placed the slip of paper into my hand with the others, letting the weight of her palm rest on my mine for a moment. "This way you won't have to explain everything to your family doctor until you're ready."

There was an odd changing of the guard as Nurse Jane returned and, with a curt nod, the doctor left. Turning her back to me, Nurse Jane went about finishing up and sealing my rape kit while I slipped back into my clothes, fumbling a little with the new numbness between my legs.

"Sorry about leaving you with the doctor earlier. Normally we wouldn't have you on your own for that exam." She paused, and I noticed her shoulders rising to settle against her earlobes. "We had another young girl come in with a similar story, so I wanted to be the one to speak with her."

I'd heard what she'd said. Another woman had been assaulted, and now she too was here to get help. In fact, the girl was probably across the hall in the opposite exam room, blocked by gurneys and IVs. I wondered if this was how every day unfolded here—women in and women out—and if that contributed to Nurse Jane's detachment, her predisposition to make excuses for the predators who sent women to her waiting rooms.

Shaking off the thought, I reached for my purse as Nurse Jane moved to stand between me and the door. It was less an attempt to block my way than it was an effort to secure my attention.

Dipping her head to look into my eyes, she asked, "I know you weren't comfortable reporting last night after it happened, but are you absolutely positive you don't want to speak with an officer?"

I hesitated long enough for her to step around me and grab a handful of pamphlets from the wall rack. "Okay, that's alright." Shoving them into my hands, she hooked her finger gently under my chin and raised it just slightly, "There is no statute of limitations in Canada on sexual assault. You don't have to make a decision now. But just know the longer you wait, the harder it will be."

I knew she meant that the longer I waited to report, the harder it would be to get a conviction. But something in the back of my mind flinched, and I knew the little pit bull was still there. But she was tired now, and afraid we would forever be defending our innocence—whether to a jury or to ourselves.

CHAPTER 4

Sex and Lies

BABY CARROTS INTO THE SANDWICH BAGGIES. DON'T FORGET *spoons for the yogurt. Sandwich on top so the bread isn't crushed by their juice. Zip up the lunch bags. Tuck them into the front pouch of their schoolbags. Don't forget water. And extra socks. Somehow, they always need extra socks.*

The two weeks after the assault had been painstakingly slow. The bruises under my eye and the thumbprints on my arms had begun to fade, and the tenderness between my legs was almost nonexistent thanks mostly to the painkillers. But there was one thing that continued to grow. Like forgotten ivy on exposed brick, the memories of the assault began to creep and climb into nearly every crevice of my mind. Especially at night, when it was dark and there was so little to distract me.

Which was why I was focusing so hard on going through the motions of parenthood. Why I took an extra-long time to tie a shoelace or let the bath water grow cold before plucking them out and into the warmth of a dry towel. I was positive that if I didn't put on a show, they might know how much I was struggling.

Of course, it was foolish to think Joe wasn't aware. It was impossible to hide from him that I wasn't sleeping. I'd lost count of how many nights he would wake to find me sitting on the edge of the bed in the dark, rocking back and forth, willing the nightmares to go away. I would jump at every unexpected sound, become irritated with the slightest change in our routine, and I refused to be alone whenever possible. In fact, that was one of the reasons I'd returned to work at the yoga studio just a few days after my visit to the hospital. The idea of being home alone during the day, even with the sunlight to keep me company, was too much.

As I lined the boys' schoolbags up neatly beside the front door, a soft buzzing came from my cell phone, left to charge on the kitchen counter. Having a few minutes before I was supposed to shoo the kids out the door for their short walk to school, I hurried over to check the notification.

10/11/17
MISSED CALL – 905-755-****

It was a familiar number. Not because I knew the caller but because it had called nearly five times a day, every day for the last week. An unsettling lump formed in the back of my throat. Trying to push it back down, I returned the phone to its charger and started toward the hall to call the boys.

Before I could even round the corner, the sound of thudding footsteps on the hard wood floors caused me to freeze. And when Declyn leapt into view, his voice still high with youth and his floppy brown hair falling over his green eyes, his playful squeals sent me crumpling into a hunched position on the floor.

A moment later, I realized he'd simply been attempting to give me a harmless scare, but instead of laughing, my voice came out shrill and scathing. "What the fuck, Declyn? Why would you try to scare me like that? That was awful! Don't ever do that again." I punctuated the last five words harshly. And immediately regretted it.

His face fell in a way I'd never seen but had always feared. Discipline was a staple in our household. In fact, many of our friends teased that we were too strict. That the helicopter parenting method was the way to go, but as someone who'd lacked structure and security as a child, I knew exactly how important it was. But this wasn't the face of a child who had just been scolded. This was the face of a child who was afraid of their mother.

"I'm so sorry." Shuffling toward him on my knees, I pulled him into an embrace, his body understandably stiff against mine. "I'm so sorry, buddy. Mommy shouldn't have yelled like that. I guess I just scare easy." Leaning back, I held his shoulders and looked into his now slightly less timid eyes. "You are so good at sneaking up on me! I didn't even hear you coming. Maybe next time you can try it on your brothers, okay?" He nodded and waited patiently until I kissed his forehead and released him.

Wiping a hand across my brow, which was now damp with sweat, I heard shuffling to my right. Joe was standing down the hall, Milo and Cash in front of him, gauging my next move. I rose from the floor and straightened my shirt, reaching out to give each of the boys a kiss on his head as they wandered past in search of their backpacks.

Joe followed them, stopping to place a hand on my shoulder and steady the trembling I hadn't realized had begun. "How about I walk the kids to school today?"

"But you have to get to that new job site, and you're already staying up late on Tuesdays and Thursdays to pick me up from the yoga studio so I don't have to drive alone," I began to protest.

He leaned down and pressed his lips against mine. It was tender enough to calm some of the chaos tumbling around inside me. Not forever, but for the moment.

Joe helped Milo slip his arms into the straps of his bag and tugged a hat onto his head before shooing them all out the door. "Make a coffee. Sit and catch your breath. We'll talk when I get back."

I was rarely one to follow instead of lead, but there was a strange comfort in doing as Joe said. Waiting for the door to close behind them, then making my way to the kitchen, then pouring another cup of hot black coffee and shuffling to the bedroom, where I sat on the bed and quietly sipped from my mug. It felt like autopilot. As if Joe had typed in the coordinates and I'd followed the simple instructions to a safe destination.

It was easy. Well, it was easier than navigating the crossed wires and missing roadmaps of my own mind. But I didn't like the lack of control. I hadn't felt in charge of my body or actions or emotions in weeks, and regardless of whether it was Joe in the driver's seat or something more sinister, I didn't want to be a passenger in my own life any longer.

Twenty minutes or so passed before I heard the front door open and then close softly. Before my body could jump at the sound, I'd registered that it was Joe coming home. A small win. Without a word, he padded into the room and sat beside me on the bed. We both avoided looking at each other, a situation reminiscent of the years when our marriage had been in trouble and we'd spent many hours in silence, willing the other to say something.

After an uncomfortable minute, Joe noticed the stack of pamphlets from the hospital on the dresser where I'd discarded them after my visit. He pulled them into his lap and started to flip through them.

"You can't keep living like this," he said, his voice a little sad. "You are so afraid and obviously miserable and I don't know how to help you. I just want you to be you again."

There was comfort in his concern. Having spent the majority of my life as the one in charge of everyone else's emotions, it occasionally felt good to have someone worried about mine. But along with his concern, I couldn't ignore the quiver in his voice that made me think there might be even the tiniest bit of pity there too, and it irritated me. No one wanted to be pitied, and I certainly hadn't asked for it.

I ran my thumb around the lip of my mug to wipe away the coffee stains before snapping my reply. "Maybe if you weren't going out every weekend with a new woman, I wouldn't feel so alone and afraid." Joe tilted his head, probably wondering if I was being serious or snarky. I was being snarky. "Sorry, that wasn't necessary. I guess I just feel unhinged when you're not here, even if you're only out for a couple hours. I need you right now."

"I know you do, and that's why I've been trying to be here whenever I can." He gripped the pamphlets tightly in his hands. "Are you thinking you want to go back to monogamy?"

Without hesitation I shook my head. "No, not at all. I don't think I could ever go back to that. I just think we should put a pause on seeing other people." This time I raised my eyes to meet his. "I don't ever want to go back to the way we were, but right now I need all of you. I'm sorry."

He scooted closer on the bed and draped an arm around me, "Don't be sorry, seriously." He hugged me close. "We'll make it work until you want to revisit it. But I still think it would help to talk to someone about what happened."

Joe held out one of the pamphlets. "WOMEN'S CENTRE OF YORK REGION" was typed in a big, bold, purple font that took up the majority of the cover page. Inside were softly italicized testimonials from anonymous past patients and neatly organized details on how to contact them for counselling and trauma therapy.

I picked at the edges of the glossy paper. "I don't know. The only time I've gone to therapy was because we were on the brink of divorce."

He smiled. "True, but it worked out for the best, didn't it?"

It had. Those sessions had saved our marriage, and so, in its own way, had adopting non-monogamy. But leaning into that lifestyle and the power it gave me in our relationship, as well as my own confidence and sexuality, had also led me directly into the hands of a predator. A big part of me felt stupid for not predicting the consequences of my actions, and selfish for thinking I deserved help in the aftermath.

Of course, when I'd first walked into our marriage counsellor's office three years earlier, I'd felt stupid and selfish too. Stupid for not noticing Joe's infidelities sooner, and selfish for seriously considering walking away.

* * *

"Was it the sex or the lies?"

Joe and I sat side by side on a stiff couch in the office of Dr. Sheppard, a marriage counsellor who specialized in infidelity and non-traditional relationship-building. We had only been married four years at that point, together for seven, and it felt like failure to be already seeking professional help. But a close friend—one who'd had his own battle with infidelity and repairing the wounds it caused to his marriage—had recommended Dr. Sheppard and giving it one last chance. I went along with the idea, even though it seemed as if all I did was give people chances, and every time they made me regret it.

We were there because Joe had cheated. Again. And this time it wasn't just a romp in the back seat of his work truck with an ex-girlfriend, when he was frustrated over our fighting about the wedding we couldn't afford or the pregnancy we hadn't expected. It wasn't the dancer who did more than entertain him with her rhythm at a friend's bachelor party when I was still carrying more than fifty pounds of baby weight and felt disgusted at the idea of being touched. It wasn't even because of the raunchy text messages he had been sending to multiple other women during those times when I would leave him home with the kids while I ran on the treadmill for hours in an effort to feel fit and confident again.

This time it had been a full-blown affair. Text messages and emails confirmed my suspicions that he had been doing a little bit more than working when he was sent out west from his job in the Maritimes and left me for six weeks. Alone and lonely.

To anyone who hasn't experienced a partner straying, it seems ridiculous to suggest you can categorize cheating by severity. Any unfaithfulness is unacceptable, right? To some, yes. To others, it's easy to excuse a hand that roamed too far or a night filled with regrets after too many drinks. Because the truth is people fuck up.

My father fucked up; so did my mother. My sister fucked up almost daily when we were younger. Even my grandmother, whom I placed on a pedestal even long after she'd passed away when I was in high school, had fucked up by staying with my alcoholic grandfather. But seldom did people fuck up intentionally, or, at the very least, they didn't do it maliciously. And it was because of that distinction that I'd been able to forgive Joe's earlier indiscretions as the acts of an immature, self-conscious young man.

But this time was different. We weren't kids anymore. During the time he'd been gone, I'd been home with our three-month-old son, a toddler, and my oldest, who had just started school. I was juggling their care while watching my nephew during the day to try to make up for what my maternity leave wasn't providing. Sure, I had my family and even my in-laws, who would visit from time to time, but every night I went to bed alone and every morning I woke up alone. The loneliness was nearly as crushing as the towering banks of snow that barricaded us into our home that winter. Truth was, I'd be lonely in our marriage for a while even before Joe left, and finding out that while I'd been alone he'd happily found someone to keep him company was the last straw.

"The lies." The words left my mouth before I'd even really thought them. Dr. Sheppard made a note on her paper. Joe fidgeted beside me.

We'd been seeing Dr. Sheppard once a week, every week, for two months, unpacking and rehashing the highs and very low lows of our marriage. She wanted us to start from the beginning when we'd fallen in love so quickly and become a family unit even though neither of us was really equipped to do so. His ingrained programming to repress any negative feelings instead of sharing them, which lead to outbursts and distancing himself. My obsessive need to be reassured every minute of every day that Joe was with me because he loved me and not just for the kids. I nagged; he pushed me away. I resented him; he resented me for resenting him. According to Dr. Sheppard, neither of us had healthy communication skills.

"Have you ever lied to Joe?" she asked, sitting back in her chair and crossing one leg over the other.

"No, of course not." I was appalled she would even think about turning the blame on me. I was not the reason we were here.

"Really?" Joe turned toward me. "Then why did I have to find out you're bisexual from the search history on our computer?"

The string of expletives I wanted to hurl at him stuck in my throat.

"Or when you were still talking to your ex-boyfriend six months after we started dating and you lied about accidentally running into him when I saw you two having a coffee?"

"We were just friends," I snapped back.

Joe rolled his eyes.

Dr. Sheppard sat forward. "Let's circle back to the first thing you mentioned, Joe. How did it make you feel when you found out about Eden's sexuality? Did she outright lie about it?"

Joe sank back into the couch. "No. I mean, I never asked her about it. Of course, we'd talked about having a threesome once or twice, but it never happened. So I just assumed she wasn't into women."

"But my lie didn't hurt anyone." I scooted to the edge of the seat, elbows resting on my knees. "It's not like I've been able to even explore how I feel about women. We've been together since I was twenty-two, and before that I hadn't realized it was more than a passing feeling."

"In the interest of fairness, you had the opportunity to explore it when Joe suggested bringing another partner into the bedroom," Dr. Sheppard said. "What stopped you?"

I glanced over at Joe; I could tell he wanted to know as well. "'Cause I knew I would be jealous. I'd go crazy with jealousy. The only reason the conversation came up was because I'd already caught him cheating a couple times and I thought maybe if we invested more time into what we both wanted physically that it would keep his attention on me."

"But instead, I suggested we bring someone else in." Joe hung his head, his voice barely a whisper. "I'm such a fucking asshole."

A tense moment or two passed before Dr. Sheppard cleared her throat. "If Joe had never cheated, if you'd had healthy trust and honesty from the start, would you have agreed to the threesome?"

I thought about it. It's not like I was a prude; I'd just never been in a position to explore any of the things I'd fantasized about.

"Probably." I stared down at my hands. "There are things I've thought about that I'd like to do or try. But I know I wouldn't be able to with someone I don't trust."

"You don't trust me?" Joe's hand crept across the cushions, stopping just before it touched mine.

"You blame me?" My hand trembled in my lap. I was still angry, but I was starting to realize the complexity of the events that had led us there.

"Can you ever trust him again?" Dr. Sheppard asked.

"Of course I can! That's all I do. Trust, have it broken, trust, have it broken. But it always ends up being on his terms."

"What if it were on your terms?" Rummaging through a pile of books under a small end table beside her chair, Dr. Sheppard pulled out a few and stacked them in her lap. "We've only been working together a few months, but from what I've gathered, the biggest issue you face is communication and dishonesty. Second to that would be the confinements of the traditional marriage structure not allowing either of you to explore your physical needs fully."

She leaned across and handed me a book, *The Ethical Slut*. Flipping it over, I read the back out loud: "The classic guide to love, sex, and intimacy beyond the limits of conventional monogamy. The authors dispel myths and show curious readers how to maintain a successful polyamorous lifestyle through open communication, emotional honesty, and safer sex practices."

"You want us to open our marriage?" Joe took the book from my hands and started flipping through it.

"I want Eden to open your marriage, and I want you to focus on rebuilding her trust by being radically honest and clearly communicating how you're feeling"—she smirked, the first sign of humour beneath her glossy professional veneer—"instead of acting out like a toddler who isn't getting enough attention from his mother."

"I'd be *allowing* him to screw other women, instead of him going behind my back to do it? Isn't that essentially rewarding him for bad behaviour?" I took the book back from Joe and held it tightly.

"No, and I'll tell you why." Dr. Sheppard pointed at the back of the book with her pen. "Polyamory or non-monogamous relationships revolve entirely around trust. Some of those relationships start from a place of trust, but since you don't currently have that, it would look a little different. In fact, it would look however you wanted it to."

"I'm sorry, I'm trying to be open here. I love this man." I looked over at Joe, who seemed as uneasy as I was with this line of conversation. "Even if he is an asshole, he's my best friend. But I'm not understanding what you're proposing."

She grinned again. "I get it. We're all raised on the happily-ever-afters and the belief there is this mythical one person meant for everyone. But that just doesn't work for some people, and that's okay. I don't think you two are failing at being married; I think traditional marriage is failing you."

"And if we decided to explore a non-traditional marriage, it would be on my terms? Like until I could trust him again, I could see other people but he couldn't? Or only if I approved of his dates?" I searched Joe's face for even the slightest hint he wouldn't be on board, that he'd push back against my taking control in our relationship. But instead, all I saw was curiosity.

"That's exactly right." Dr. Sheppard leaned forward, resting her chin on her hand. "But you would have to be a willing participant, Joe, not just playing along to make her happy. There will be a lot of work. Sometimes taking accountability for your actions is the hardest part."

I could feel his eyes on me, like when warm sunshine falls on your face through a window. Daring to meet his gaze, I felt a hiccup catch in my throat as a sob attempted to bubble up. Tears wet his cheeks, making the freckles that swept across his skin stand out. They were one of the first things I'd noticed when we'd met all those years ago.

After a moment of struggling with his vulnerability, Joe cleared his throat, reached across, and wrapped his hand around mine. He turned to Dr. Sheppard and said, "She's worth it."

CHAPTER 5

Peeling the Onion

THE FLUORESCENT LIGHTS ABOVE ME BUZZED LIKE AN ANGRY swarm of wasps. Faded grey carpet matched the walls of the narrow hallway, which was dotted with a handful of nondescript office doors. Behind one of those doors was a trauma counsellor who would be assigned to help me navigate the road to recovery after my rape. At least that's what the glossy pamphlet for the Women's Centre of York Region had said. It had taken about a week to get an appointment, and the waiting had felt like purgatory.

As I made my way down the narrow hallway, the lights above flickered at odd intervals, distracting me from the heaviness creeping into my legs with every step. It took longer than I expected to find the right door. Room 516B was unassuming, no nameplate or lacquered plaque embossed with the office's details. Just a small metal intercom situated on the wall beside the door. I double-checked the Post-it Note stuck to the front of the pamphlet, where

I'd hastily jotted the information the receptionist had given me when I'd made my appointment. The address was correct, as was the office number. So I pushed the button on the intercom and waited while my phone buzzed in my pocket. I tried to ignore it, but the vibration against my leg fell into an eerie rhythm with the humming of the florescent lights and I had to pull it out.

10/16/17 UKNOWN: Hey stranger… ;)

Glancing over my shoulder, I made sure I was still alone in the hallway. I was about to respond that they had the wrong number when a crackling came over the tiny speaker and a voice asked, "Name?"

Holding the button, I replied, "Eden Boudreau."

The voice came across again. "Have your ID and health card ready. When you hear the click, you can enter."

Click.

I turned the knob and pushed the door open. It was much heavier than expected, and I had to lean into it with my shoulder long enough to pass through. As I let it thunk closed behind me, I realized it must have been reinforced steel masquerading as a normal door. Once inside, I found myself in a small four-foot-by-four-foot vestibule with another locked door, presumably leading into the office. To my right, behind a wall of scuffed plexiglass, was a young receptionist with a kind smile. Even with her approachable demeanour easing my tension slightly, the air in the small space still felt stale and seemed to catch in my throat.

As I stared blankly through the foggy barrier, the receptionist continued to smile and pointed at the small slot near the bottom.

"Oh yes, sorry," I stammered. Fumbling with my ID cards, I slid them through the slot to her waiting hands. After a few clicks of her keyboard she slid them back.

"You'll hear another click and then you can enter through this door, take a left, and have a seat on the couch. Someone will be with you shortly." Her smile remained genuine and welcoming, but for the first time I noticed she looked tired. The image struck me as an odd juxtaposition, but when I imagined the strength it must take to work in this field—patching up the wounded women who came through these doors and sending them back out into the world, much like medics on the front lines of a war—I could understand how the exhaustion would show from time to time.

Click.

I pulled open the second door, this one far less heavy and foreboding. Beyond it was a maze-like office with cubicles and closet-sized rooms scattered haphazardly throughout the space. To the left, where I had been directed, was a corner with a mildly tattered leather couch, a fake fern, and a wall full of brochures. Taking a seat across from the overflowing rack, I wondered how and when these small folded pieces of paper had become the go-to form of communication for mental health assistance.

Scanning the office as I balanced on the edge of the couch, I noticed the workers were all women of varying ages scurrying to and from each other's desks as mountains of paperwork threatened to spill from their folders. Even though the overall atmosphere was calm and welcoming, hearing the snippets of hushed conversations behind closed doors, the hurried tapping of heels on tile, and the constant refilling of coffee mugs grated against my already frayed nerves. The reality that I was about to open up to yet another stranger—spill my trauma all over their lap and then ask them to help me search through it for some kind of meaning—seemed unbelievable. And completely out of character.

Click.

Another woman close to my age with two small toddlers, their arms wrapped tightly around her legs, came to sit beside me. When she'd entered, she'd been wearing a thin navy-blue veil, that I recognized as a hijab, pulled tight against her face. It covered her hair and encircled her face. But as she sat and hoisted her daughter into her lap, the child's tiny hand grabbed hold of the fabric and tugged. The veil fell just slightly, enough to reveal a cluster of dark purple bruises skirting her hairline and ringing her jaw. Before I could stop it, my breath made a sick sucking sound. Immediately, she fumbled to resecure the fabric, and I knew I had not only offended her modesty but her privacy as well.

I looked away, the very least I could do, and my eyes roamed the rack of pamphlets. Scanning them, I started to notice certain recurring words. *Safety. Domestic. Confidential. Support.* Looking around the small, highly secured office again, I saw more than just a few tired female employees. Everyone who worked there was a woman. The only male presence was that of the odd son, accompanying his battered mother.

That's when it hit me: This wasn't just a centre for rape victims. It was a safe space for all victims of violent acts—sexual, domestic, professional, or otherwise. I can imagine the average person would feel immense comfort knowing there was such a place for women who often had nowhere else to turn. But me? I immediately felt like a fraud, a leech, like I was wasting everyone's time and energy having even walked through those doors. There were women here, like the one beside me cradling her daughter, who had suffered so much longer and under more severe circumstances than I had. And here I was taking the space of someone who needed it more. I stood to leave.

"Mrs. Boudreau?" A whisper of a woman with dark eyes and glossy skin of the same hue came around the corner just then, a folder tucked neatly under one arm and a mug of tea in the opposite hand. If I had to guess, she was likely a few years younger than me. Early thirties. No wedding ring. No fine lines around her eyes or wispy grey hairs, so probably no kids. Of everyone I'd met in this place so far, she seemed the most at ease. Which somehow made me even more anxious.

I considered walking out. Pretending I was someone else. Avoiding her gaze and fleeing like the chickenshit I was. This wasn't some patronizing holy martyr bullshit going on in my head; it was a feeling of overwhelming guilt at taking from those whom I believed deserved the help more than I did.

My whole childhood had been one handout after another, maybe the occasional hand up, but always overflowing generosity that I knew I would never be able to adequately pay back. So as an adult, I'd sworn to never take more than my fair share, ever. Such is the way of the kid who grew up poor. But there was something about this woman standing in front of me, patiently waiting with her round cheeks still soft with leftover youth, back straight, shoulders high, and neither a smile nor a frown. She wasn't expecting me to run, but she wasn't pressuring me to stay either. As if she was giving me the choice. And as someone who'd had that right taken from her so recently, I realized it was enough to make me want to see it through. To choose what I did next with my own life. Maybe even to make her proud of my choice.

I nodded, and she smiled.

"Great, I'm Farrah." Extending her arm in the direction of a small hall, she took the lead and guided me into an office. Based on the layout of the interior waiting area, I hadn't expected plush, expansive counselling rooms with velvet fainting couches or a mimosa cart. But this room could easily have doubled as a storage closet where they kept extra rolls of toilet paper and the few dollar-store Halloween decorations they would put up soon. The far-too-bright white walls were completely bare except for one window, which looked out on the parking lot's dumpster collection. The rest of the office was decorated with a generic filing cabinet, a printer, two plastic chairs, and a plain white desk that sat between us. Everything in the room felt stiff, including the chair I perched in across from Farrah. Shifting my weight from the back to the front and back again, I tried to slow my mind down from barrelling full-speed into anxiety.

While I was already well on my way to a panic attack, Farrah took a moment to situate herself. Flipping through the pages sandwiched neatly in the folder, she hummed so quietly I almost didn't hear her over the buzzing of the overhead lights. I gazed up at them and thought how they were too bright for the dark conversations that happened in this room. Once Farrah had caught herself up, she cleared her throat and took a long sip of her tea. Her casual approach should have been reassuring, but it was only irritating my frayed nerves.

Finally, she sat back in her chair and pushed the folder aside. "So the attending doctor at the hospital sent over all their notes from your visit. But why don't you tell me why you are here, in your own words."

I felt as if I were hovering over the seat of my chair, ready to make a run for it, again. Going over the details of my assault for Nurse Jane had seemed practical. Rationally, I needed medical care, and to receive it, I had to be open about what had happened. But spewing my emotional vomit all over this poor woman's lap felt so self-indulgent, especially considering who waited outside. I fidgeted with the hem of my sweater. This seemed somehow harder than every hurdle that had come before it.

She waited. I stalled. She took another long sip of tea. I exhaled and finally started to talk. Twenty minutes later I took another breath.

"Okay." Farrah put down her mug and shuffled the papers within the folder until she found a blank page. She jotted a few notes and then folded her hands on the desktop. "You've been through a lot in the last little while."

I nodded, an odd emptiness settling in my gut. Even in my peak rebellious youth, I'd rarely drank to get drunk, but there was the odd time when too much whiskey or wine left me emptying the contents of my stomach on a dark sidewalk after the bar had closed. This reminded me of the moment immediately after that, when you felt completely empty. Except no relief followed.

"It hasn't been ideal, no." I picked at a loose nubbin of wool on the hem of my sweater. "But I'm sure you've heard a lot worse before."

"There is no better or worse when it comes to traumatic experiences." Farrah leaned forward. "You know what happened to you was not only not okay but incredibly unfair, right?" Her dark eyes searched my face. I had the feeling she was looking for some sign I agreed, but I wasn't sure I did.

Fairness had always felt more like an opinion than a truth for me. Was it fair when another preschooler, the boy who threw rocks at neighbourhood cats, reached under my skirt and pawed at my panties when I was four? Probably not, but according to his mother, I should have been wearing tights if I didn't want to attract unwanted attention.

Was it fair when I kissed a boy for the first time behind the bank of mailboxes down the street from my junior high and, instead of the truth, he told everyone I gave him a blowjob, causing them all to whisper *slut* as they passed my locker for the rest of the year? Nope, but according to the other girls in my grade, I should have known people would talk if I put myself in that position.

Or what about when I went through a rough period after becoming a mother in my early twenties, wanting to be the rebellious and reckless one for once. Was it fair that a man twice my size and significantly less intoxicated followed me into a bedroom during a house party while I drunkenly searched for my coat and then grabbed me, pinning me against a wall by my throat when I politely declined his advances? The so-called friends I was partying with agreed it may not have been fair, but in their opinion, "That's what you get for hanging out with those kinds of people."

What it came down to was this: Fairness only applied when you could be completely absolved of any fault in a situation. And when you're a woman, that's a rare occurrence.

When Farrah failed to pull a concrete agreement out of me on the question of fairness, she continued in a different vein. "Well, I'm not here to convince you of anything, but I do hope by the end of our sessions you'll start to see that for yourself." She clicked her pen and made a few more notations. All I could manage was a slow nod. My entire body felt as if it were being pulled into the floor and my mind was foggy with exhaustion. I hoped I would too.

"Okay, so we've established how you got here, but not necessarily why. Why are you here today, Eden?" She tilted her head, inquisitive but not patronizing.

I stared at a chip on the edge of the desk, a notch that gained depth the longer I looked at it. Farrah cleared her throat.

"I can't sleep." Using my nail, I picked at the chip, white paint flaking away. "And if I do, it's never for long."

She sipped her tea and thought about that. "And what wakes you up?"

I chuffed a morbid laugh. "Everything." Another chip of paint came away and lodged under my nail. "The slightest sound. My husband rolling over in bed. Nightmares. The dark." I sighed and looked up to find Farrah watching me closely. "Every single thing."

Leaning forward, she cradled her mug between the palms of her hands. "You mentioned nightmares. Could you expand on that."

Shit. I'd really hoped she wouldn't zero in on that one. Why couldn't we tackle something easier? Wear noise-cancelling headphones or make Joe sleep on the couch. Expanding on the nightmares was like uncoiling a sleeping snake. At some point you would come to the head, and that's where the teeth were.

The nightmares weren't necessarily new since the assault; they were just significantly worse. I'd been experiencing them since as far back as I could remember. It was like my mind took all the chaos and torment I suppressed during the day and wove it into an off-brand Salvador Dali painting at night. When I was younger, the dreams had featured snippets of arguments between my parents or bullying at school, threading their way through desolate landscapes and claustrophobic spaces. Now they were far more rooted in reality—like a highlight reel of my assault that had been burned at the edges and translated into a dead language. I knew exactly what was happening and what would happen, only it also seemed foreign or displaced. How was I supposed to put that into words without sounding completely crazy?

"Most of the time they're just flashbacks to the assault. But these sort of warped versions." I looked up briefly and Farrah nodded, urging me to go on. "I don't always remember all the details when I wake up, but I do remember how they feel."

Her pen scratched hurriedly across the paper. "And how is that?"

I hesitated, unsure how open to be, worried it would just sign my ticket to a room with padded walls.

Resigned, I looked up at the ceiling. The lights seemed even brighter now, making tears pool in the corners of my eyes. "They just seem so fucken real. Even hours after I've woken up, I can't shake that feeling. It feels like it follows me around all day."

Keeping my gaze tilted upward, I frantically blinked back the encroaching wetness on my lashes. I felt the table shift and then felt Farrah's hand, warm and firm, her fingers gently wrapping around mine. No longer able to resist, I let the tears trickle down my cheeks and meet beneath my chin before falling to pool in my lap.

Farrah's soft voice urged me back to the conversation. "Everything you've described is completely normal. Many rape victims struggle with determining what is really happening and what is a trauma memory."

"It is?" A real laugh bubbled up as I choked back a sob. "I'm sorry—I don't know why I find that funny. It's definitely not funny. I guess it's just funny that I'm not actually crazy."

She smiled, one side of her small mouth rising and forming a dimple in her cheek. "It is." She sat back and flipped through her papers, pulling out a photocopied page. Sliding it across the table, she pointed to the bold black text at the top. "It sounds like what you're experiencing is PTSD—post-traumatic stress disorder."

My face screwed up in confusion. "Isn't that what soldiers get when they come home from war?"

"Yes, but it's also much more common in domestic and sexual violence victims than people realize."

That word—*victim*. It had come up twice now. It made me feel so helpless, so broken, and fragile. The girl who'd once stood toe-to-toe with bullies and bad men would be fuming at even the insinuation that she was a victim. But she wasn't here anymore; she hadn't protected us when we needed it. So maybe I was more of a victim than I'd known.

"I think that might be a bit dramatic. It's just nightmares." I swiped at the wetness on my cheeks, angry at myself for allowing such a pathetic display of vulnerability. "Yeah, I'm more jumpy than usual, and I can't walk through my house without every light on, but I've never been a fan of the dark. Nobody is."

I saw Farrah's body shift in a way that made me think she was reconsidering her approach. She pulled another sheet from her folder and placed it in front of me. "PTSD isn't always what you see in movies and TV shows. It doesn't always manifest as cowering when a car backfires, or crying into a bottle of rum whenever you're alone." She pointed to the page in front of me, which showed a diagram of the human brain. "It is your brain's natural response to trauma. It's how it knows to protect you against further harm."

"So my brain is just constantly assuming I'm going to get attacked again?" I pulled the paper close and studied the diagram.

School had never been a cakewalk, but not because I wasn't intelligent. I simply didn't learn the way others did. The words skipped across the pages of books, and math problems felt like ancient languages I would never understand. And the frustration that came with not keeping up with my peers depleted my self-worth even further. Later in life I would be diagnosed with ADHD, but as I sat across from Farrah trying to understand how this melon-sized mass of nerves and tissue could possibly protect me, I wished I had paid more attention in eighth-grade biology.

Farrah pointed at the brain. "Memories aren't just relegated to sad or happy. Traumatic memories don't just remind you that something very bad happened—something that resulted in you being hurt. They serve as a sort of alarm system. So when your brain detects something that correlates with a traumatic memory, like sounds or smells or even just the dark"—she pointed to a paragraph below the diagram—"it sends your body into fight, flight, or freeze mode regardless of whether there is actual danger present."

"So my brain is gaslighting me?" I looked up from the paper, searching to see if my attempt at morbid humour had lightened the mood at all. To my surprise, I found a smile on Farrah's face. Maybe I wasn't the only one who had some unhealthy coping mechanisms.

"No, because it's not trying to make you feel guilty about being afraid. It's trying to keep you alive."

As Farrah shuffled through papers in another folder among the stacks in the filing cabinet, I went back to the paragraph on the sheet where it mentioned fight, flight, or freeze mode.

I turned the page toward her and pointed. "I've heard of the first two, but what is freeze mode?"

She left the drawer slightly ajar and sat back in her chair, crossing her arms. "That's the technical term for when your brain and body become frozen in order to make it out of the dangerous situation alive. Some people liken it to a possum playing dead."

Slowly lowering the paper, I let my gaze wander to the window behind Farrah. In the grey sky beyond the glass there were three birds, one larger than the rest, dipping and flipping through the air in a primal show of prey and predator.

"That's what I did. I just laid there like a fucking possum and let him do whatever he wanted. I let it happen." Suddenly, it felt as if a battering ram had slammed into my chest. I struggled to breath and sweat trickled down the small of my back.

Farrah didn't make any sudden moves, but her hands fell to her lap and she leaned forward. "You did what you had to do to survive, Eden."

For the first time since the attack, I could feel something akin to anger. The fear and anxiety I'd been drowning in were disorienting, but this—this emotion felt like wet cement filling my chest and crushing my lungs beneath its weight. "They won't care how big he was. That even when I tried to push him off me, I couldn't. That when he punched me over and over, I knew if I screamed for help it would only get worse. All they'll see is a married woman, getting fucked in a dark parking lot, regretting it and then crying rape."

"Is that what happened?" Farrah asked.

I could recognize the signs of a panic attack in my sleep. They had plagued me since well before I could even spell *anxiety*. So as I rested my elbows on my knees, my head in my hands, I tried to find my breath and my voice. Farrah didn't rush to my side, but she stood and walked around the desk, waiting beside my chair.

I whispered, "No."

Her voice was a little deeper, firmer now: "Is that what happened?"

I knew she wasn't interrogating me; she believed me. But she needed *me* to believe it too. Tears dripped from my cheeks and I watched them disappear into the mousey green carpet beneath my feet.

I took a deep breath and answered, "No."

A moment of silence passed, and then there was a soft noise beside me. Farrah had slid a paper cup of water in front of me on the desk. I had no idea when or where she'd gotten it, but I didn't care. My shaking hand wrapped around the cup, the cool water inside touching my lips and slipping down my throat. It gave me something to focus on other than the panic, a distraction. My limbs were weak with exhaustion and I strained to keep my head up.

Maybe I had been looking for attention. Maybe after growing up in the shadow of my parents' divorce, or my older sister's headlong sprint into addiction, maybe I did want the spotlight on myself for a moment. After years of my husband's infidelity, devoting myself to being the best wife and mother I could be, was it really so wrong to want someone who put me on a pedestal and showered me in affection. *But did that negate my innocence? Did that automatically mean I was asking for it?*

I tried to summon a chuckle. "So one and done, right? I'm cured?" There was that morbid humour again.

Again, Farrah returned my grin. "I wish it were that easy." Returning to her seat, she pointed to a group of concentric circles on one of the sheets she'd placed on the desk. "Healing trauma is a bit like unwrapping an onion. You can't just start on the top layer, the most recent trauma, acknowledge it and walk away." She moved her finger over the circles from the outside in. "You have to unwrap every layer, one at a time, dealing with the most prominent issues first and working your way to the root. It's the only way to truly heal. Stopping midway can lead to revictimization or further mental health struggles, like addiction or suicide."

"I hate onions." I took another sip of the water.

"We all do." She shuffled the paperwork from my file and neatly tucked it back inside, a subliminal signal to reassure me we were done for today. "It's a process, but I'm dedicated to helping you heal. And we'll get through it together."

I still felt guilty for needing help. But another part of me, the part that had waited at the end of the bed for her mother to wake up, was happy to finally have someone willing to be there.

With a handful of tissues and another glass of water, we made our way to the front desk, where I scheduled my next appointment and thanked Farrah. The woman who had been waiting with her children was gone, and a small part of me was relieved at the thought that she might be in one of the tiny offices, finding her own sort of comfort.

Exhaustion pulled at my heels as I left the office, but there was also a new brightness in the corners of my vision. Almost as if some of the gloom had finally lifted. I carried that with me all the way out to my car, where Joe waited for me.

"How was it?" He smiled, but I could see a hint of hesitation behind it. He was so desperate to have the person he used to know back, and there was nothing I wanted to give him more.

"Surprisingly cathartic. I'm sure not every session will be that way, but it feels like a good place to start."

Joe reached across and placed his hand over mine, giving it a gentle squeeze. "As long as it's helping."

As we drove home, the autumn colours that had felt muted before took on a wash of warmth. I supposed this was what it would be like to describe hope to someone who had never known it; lately, I hadn't been sure that I remembered the notion. It was liberating. But as my phone started buzzing in my pocket, the worry returned. Hope was such a delicate thing, like the wing of a bird, and it could be crushed so easily.

CHAPTER 6

Triggered

ANXIOUSLY TAPPING THE END OF MY PEN ON THE HARDWOOD DESK
that took up half of the crescent-shaped reception area of the yoga
studio, I cradled my cell phone between my shoulder and chin
while listening to Kami listing all the ways my boisterous nephew
had been trying her patience that week.

During classes, while the soft cascading of teachers' voices
would drift down the halls and the subtle scent of sage would tickle
my nose, I was usually tasked with answering phone calls, respond-
ing to client emails, organizing client membership contracts, and
following up on any overdue payments. There was usually some task
to complete, which was part of the appeal for my out-of-control
locomotive of a mind. But when it was late and the last class of the
night was underway—like tonight—there wasn't much left to do
other than twiddle my thumbs.

Recently, I'd taken advantage of the odd moment here and
there to call Kami and distract myself from the barrage of calls

from unknown numbers that were now accompanied by text messages that increased in frequency and nastiness each day. I never answered or replied, and had even started to block the numbers. But as soon as I'd stopped one, another showed up. Even though I didn't engage with the sender, I couldn't help but read the texts. They varied between coaxing and flirtatious on the one hand, and venomous and threatening on the other. It all felt too familiar and overwhelming.

"How easy is it to trace a phone number?" I asked my sister.

Kami paused for a minute, and I heard what sounded like tapping. "About a thirty-second Google search, it looks like." She'd sent a link to my cell phone for a website where you could trace any number with the owner's name to see if it matched what was publicly known. "Of course, it probably only works if the number isn't private or one of those spoof services."

I could hear her take a long drag on a cigarette, and I pictured her sitting on her balcony with a ginger cat perched in her lap and a Player's king-size between her long fingers. I had no idea if that was what she still smoked, but it was part of the nostalgia I'd cultivated from when we were younger. It was oddly comforting.

"Hmmm…" I mumbled into the phone as I tapped the keyboard on our work computer, inputting some of the numbers in my call log.

Kami's concerned voice came over the line. "You okay?"

I tried to gather myself. "Yeah, I'm okay. Just distracted."

"I've noticed. Tell me honestly, kiddo, what's going on with you."

I paused. Then cleared my throat and said, "I was raped."

There was a hesitation on the other end and then she replied, "Fuck."

"Yeah." I chuckled in a way only a sister would know meant *Yeah, this is so fucked up and I can't believe I didn't tell you sooner either.*

"Did you go to the cops?"

"No."

Kami didn't ask why. She had been born in the 70s and raised in the 80s, peek slasher-film era and a time that was robust with serial killers, rapists, kidnappers and violent domestic abuse. She never spoke openly about it, but I knew she'd seen her fair share of friends try to leave bad situations, had maybe even tried to leave her own, and then watched as the justice system barely lifted a finger to help. Victims and survivors fell into this sort of outcast group of loners who had to fend for themselves, lest they be a burden on society. Which never made much sense considering we were one in three, or 80 percent, or twice as likely—whichever statistic you chose to believe. It's like we all knew the way things went, even if it was awful.

We didn't have time to get any deeper into the conversation before the sound of the yoga room doors caught my attention and I had to hurriedly say goodbye. Clients with happy, zenned-out faces started rounding the corner into the reception area. Like flicking a switch, I turned on a smile and chatted with a few regulars about postures and *pranayama*. The teacher, Janine, an older woman with waves of bright blond hair and arms painted with sleeves of tattoos like my own, took her place behind the reception desk alongside me.

She and I had grown close during the time I had been working there, despite her being my senior by more than a few years. In between classes we would chat about meaningless nonsense, like which housewife should get the boot from the New York franchise, or we'd vent about deeper topics, including our struggles, past and present, in relationships.

When I was a kid, I'd had no problem making friends. Most of us managed to do so when we were shoved together into classes of twenty or thirty other toddling, still-forming humans. But as I got older I became more aware of the differences between me and my classmates. They knew I didn't have money for fancy jeans or a new book bag, that my house wasn't as clean as theirs when we'd have sleepovers, that my family yelled much more than theirs did.

And so, to pre-empt what I assumed was inevitable embarrassment, I started to pull away from friend groups and keep to myself. Over the years, I would occasionally go through periods where I craved more social interaction. During those times, I'd

begrudgingly insert myself into the most accepting fringe group—
the skater kids, the punk bands, the bar stars. But eventually, when
my priorities shifted from booking spring break trips to Cancun
to booking Mommy-and-Me play dates at the library, my drive to
keep seeking out friendships faded.

At work though, it was easier. It was sort of like preschool all
over again, when you're paired up and have no real choice but to
bond together against the overlords. Back then, the overlords were
the teachers; now, they were the students. As Janine and I waited for
the last of those students to trickle out, we chatted and laughed. The
odd student would join us, or just proclaim an exuberant farewell.
From the outside, all of it must have looked lovely. Heartwarming,
even. Inside, it felt like I was on autopilot. There were no actual feelings correlated to the actions or situations; I was just going through
the motions. And this wasn't just happening at work. When I'd drop
the kids off at school, during play dates at the park, bumping into
neighbours in the grocery aisle: It was all just an act. One I was
becoming very good at—too good.

"Alright, the hot room is all shut down and the bathrooms
are tidy. Anything else you need help with before we go?" Janine
strutted around the corner from the men's changing room, her crop
top and curve-hugging leggings accentuating every muscle she'd
worked so hard for. She looked entirely comfortable in this space
and with her role in it. A few months ago, I probably would have
too. But things were so different now.

My mother used to tease me that I was the pretty one, and my
sister had regularly chastised her male friends for fawning over me
when she was forced to pick me up after school. Nothing about that
attention appealed to me. The idea of having so many eyes focused
on me, not out of admiration but infatuation, never sat right in my
gut. Even as a young adult, an age when many young women begin
to go out of their way to attract the attention of men, the spotlight
always felt a little too hot.

But since the assault, the spotlight of the male gaze—of any
gaze, really—was unbearable, and I did everything I could to avoid

it. I'd coloured my platinum blond hair the darkest, plainest shade of brown. All form-fitting or revealing clothes had been replaced with baggy, oversized outfits. Heels were obsolete, especially now that Joe could no longer fit being my chauffeur into his schedule. Sneakers were a staple, and a pair of black Doc Martens were always in the back seat of my car. Taking one of those to the shin would at least slow someone down.

"No, I think that's everything. I'm just finishing up the cash here, and then I'll be ready to close up." I counted each quarter, sliding them across the desktop and into the palm of my hand.

Janine was shrugging into her jacket when her phone buzzed. At the same time, a pair of lights blinked in the dark parking lot. The only pair left.

"Actually, is it cool if I take off now? My ride's here a few minutes early." She grabbed her bags and was stepping into her shoes before I could protest. Normally, we tried to have at least two people close the studio in the evenings, just for security's sake, but often teachers were running from one studio to the next for their classes, so it was common to let them head out early. And asking her to stay so I wasn't alone would have entailed lying—or a much longer conversation than we had time for.

I waved at her. "For sure. Have a good night!" I tried to will the calmness in my voice to not betray me with a tremble or whimper. Closing the studio was a benign routine; nothing had ever gone wrong, and there was no reason to think tonight would be any different.

Following closely behind Janine, I waited until she'd hopped into the idling car and started to pull away before locking and relocking the front door deadbolt with a satisfying *clunk*. Next, I did a thorough sweep of the studio. No one left hiding in the practice rooms, bathroom stalls or showers. I even did a cursory check of the storage closets. You know, just in case.

After checking every nook and cranny a bad guy could possibly be hiding in, I flicked off the lights and went about shutting down the computer system. For the briefest of moments as I finished closing down the studio, I actually felt good—proud that I'd handled this challenge without bolting or suffering a panic attack. With one last look around, I put my bag and cell phone on the wooden bench near the door and then sat down to stuff my feet into my sneakers and begin lacing them.

That's when I heard the buzzing.

Picking up my phone, I saw a notification from an app I didn't recognize. Instead of opening it right away, I swiped up on the screen and searched through the dancing icons for what it might be. On the very last row, behind the obligatory stocks and newspaper apps that automatically came with your operating system, was a shiny green texting app, a red dot showing five missed messages. Ah. That one. It was an app I'd downloaded the previous summer when we'd been home visiting family in Nova Scotia and my nephew, just a few months older than my youngest son, had begged me to send him messages to his new iPad this way. We'd used it maybe a handful of times before he moved on to more interesting activities like video games and terrorizing his sister.

Truthfully, I'd thought I'd deleted it, but there it was, still active and apparently with something to tell me. Thinking my nephew had reignited his pen pal passion, I clicked on the app and watched as message after message filled the text box. It wasn't my nephew. The area code was from somewhere in the Toronto region, and the messages were far from the imagination of an eight year old.

11/06/17, 9:28 PM
UNKNOWN: *If you think I won't find you, you're as stupid as you were easy.*

11/06/17, 9:32 PM
UNKNOWN: *Stop ignoring me you dumb bitch.*

11/06/17, 9:33 PM
UNKNOWN: *I saw the pics on your fb before you blocked me. Is that yoga place where you work? Not many of those near you. Remember, you told me what town you live in. Stupid bitch.*

I didn't need to look at the profile picture to know it was him. I could hear his voice in every word on that screen. His disgust, possessiveness, and spite dripped off each syllable. The messages that had come before had been taunting, leering, even a sick attempt at flirtatious, but it was clear now I had broken the number-one rule of being a woman: I'd made him mad.

Quickly, I blocked the number and set my profile so that I could only receive messages from those in my contact list. It had been almost thirty minutes since he'd sent that last message, more than enough time to make it from where he'd told me he lived to where I was. Slinging my bag over my shoulder so that the strap crossed my chest and it sat snug on my hip, I held my cell phone in one hand and my keys in the other as I hurried to shut out all the lights. Standing in the dark vestibule, I looked out into the parking lot, lit only by a handful of weak security lights placed sporadically around the plaza building. I berated myself for parking so far across the lot, beside a row of tall dark pine trees.

My mind raced back and forth between hysterics and chastising. He was just fucking with me. There was no way he was getting off inside me again, so he was getting off by screwing with my head. For some men, fear was as much a turn-on as touch. And I was letting him get what he wanted, again. Determined to not perpetuate his sick fetish any longer, I squared my shoulders, unlocked the front door, and punched the code into the alarm panel. As the last beep echoed through the empty space, indicating I had four minutes to exit and lock the door, a phone rang. Not my phone, the studio phone. Well after every student knew we were closed.

Was it unusual for someone to call after hours, having lost a water bottle or wrist watch, hoping one of the staff might be working late and be able to find their misplaced item? No, but it wasn't all that common either. And no matter how many times the rational part of my mind tried to reason with the irrational, I couldn't stop wondering if it was him. *Would he call every yoga place north of Toronto, just hoping I'd answer the phone?* At this point, I couldn't put it past him. Violating my body hadn't been enough; he was still aching for more. More pain, more trauma. Then the ringing stopped.

Taking half a second to scan the parking lot again and seeing only my car sitting alone at the far end, I made a run for it. A literal run. My feet barely touched the pavement as I bolted through the patches of darkness, nearly dropping my key fob when I reached the car. Punching the tiny button to unlock the driver's door, I slid into the seat as soon as I heard the mechanisms engage, only to slam the locks back into place once I was inside.

I released my white-knuckle grip on my cell phone and flipped it over, swiping and bringing up the call screen. Without really thinking about it, I dialled three numbers.

"911, what's your emergency?"

My breath lodged itself in my throat.

"911, do you have an emergency?"

"Hi, uh yeah, I need to report someone harassing me."

"Harassing? Are they there now?"

I scanned the dark parking lot again. "No, no. They're sending text messages. Harassing ones."

There was a heavy silence for a moment on the other end. "Do you feel you are in imminent danger currently from this person?"

"Umm, no I guess not." No other cars had come into the lot, let alone driven by since I'd left the studio.

"Then you need to call your local police department during business hours to file a complaint"—the operator paused—"if you are actually being harassed." The subtext was clear in his tone: another hysterical woman interrupting his already arduous night shift when he clearly had more serious calls to get to.

After thanking him for his time and ending the call, I sat in the silence of my car trying to slow the drumming in my chest.

I didn't even know who I was anymore. The girl who'd climbed trees higher than all the boys, who'd stood up to a drunk neanderthal trying to cop a feel under a friend's dress, who'd walked through the worst neighbourhoods at three in the morning just to make sure my sister got home safe—that girl was fearless. That girl was also gone.

Slumping back and letting my head fall against the headrest, I blinked against the tears that burned along my lashes. Suddenly, a thunking sound from the back seat caused me to yelp and spin around to see what caused it. *Rule number two: Always check the back seat.* I scanned the darkness, and when my eyes finally adjusted, there was no looming monster waiting to attack. But there was a travel mug that had evidently rolled off the seat and into the footwell when I slumped into the seat.

This weak, skittish version of myself was bad enough. But even worse was my inability to stop wondering if I was to blame for the state I found myself in. After all, I was the one who'd agreed to open our marriage, who'd continued to embrace that lifestyle long after we'd found a happy new normal. I was the one who'd agreed to go on a date with a man I didn't know. *I* didn't scream—not loud enough. *I* didn't run, or fight back. If I'd been a little stronger, a little less selfish, would I still be trembling in my car because I'd had to walk fifty feet across a dark parking lot alone?

From somewhere in the back of my mind, a distant voice screamed, *Of course you would!* I knew full well that the world wasn't made with the safety of women in mind. Every woman I knew had been harassed, followed, leered at, catcalled, or violated. It wasn't an experience unique to my life. Still, it felt impossible to shake the self-blame. It clung to me like a sticky residue no amount of scrubbing could remove.

CHAPTER 7

Want vs. Need

SITTING ACROSS THE DESK FROM FARRAH, I RAN MY SHORT, DULL nails over the skin on my arms. Not so much scratching as a subconscious scrubbing. I hadn't noticed the little habit when it started shortly after the assault. Now it would often leave faint pink trails on my skin at the end of the day where I had begun to rub it raw. I wondered if I needed to start seeing Farrah more than once a week.

"Eden?" The concerned pitch of Farrah's voice recaptured my attention.

"Yes, sorry. What were you saying?"

She took a moment to study me and then relaxed her body, sitting back in her chair and sipping her tea. "I was asking if you and Joe have any big plans for your birthday coming up? We're into November now, so it's fast approaching!"

Farrah had been encouraging me to start trying to get out of the house for more than work and grocery runs. Especially if it meant spending time on my relationship, which, if I was being honest, was already starting to show cracks.

"Not yet. I mean, I'd be happy just staying in and eating ice cream cake in bed." I fiddled with a small frayed hole that had worn itself into the knee of my jeans.

"And what would make Joe happy?" Farrah asked.

Without even looking up, I scoffed and replied, "To bring another woman home for us to have a threesome with."

Clearly not expecting this answer, Farrah doubled over, her hand cupping her chin as her mouthful of tea threatened to escape. When she'd swallowed and dabbed her wet chin with the sleeve of her shirt, she sat up straighter and grabbed her pen. Making a scribbled notation in my folder, Farrah paused for a moment and then asked, "Is that something you want? You mentioned in one of our early sessions that you'd put a pause on your non-monogamy."

When I'd first started seeing Farrah, I had given her a short briefing of our relationship and how that played into me being on a date with another man the night I was attacked. But we hadn't gone into details yet. I knew that at some point we would have to discuss the elephant in the room—whether or not I would be able to regain a healthy physical and intimate connection with my husband, let alone anyone else—but I had planned on easing her into it a little better than I just had.

"Three years ago, absolutely not." I rested my forearms on the desk between us and let the weight of my body be held up by it. "A year ago, absolutely. But now?" I let the question hang in the air between us.

"Not sure?" Farrah asked.

I nodded. "Not sure."

"Well, it sounds like you've come a long way in rebuilding trust and setting boundaries which, when you are ready to step back into intimacy, will make it a lot easier."

"It's made it easier for me, but not for him. Sometimes I wonder if it was unfair of me to ask him to stop and wait for me to be ready."

I could feel tears stinging the corners of my eyes, a familiar burning that I loathed. "What if I'm never ready? I can't do that to him."

Farrah sat back in her chair and crossed her arms over her chest, the long dark waves of her hair tucking into the folds. She watched me, this time with less empathy and more intensity. Then she asked, "Other than Joe and myself, who have you told about the assault?"

The sudden shift in conversation caught me off guard and I stumbled over my words. "The nurses at the hospital. And the doctor of course."

Farrah shook her head. "No, I mean who close to you have you told. Family? Friends?"

Confused, I racked my mind for the answer she wanted. "Well, I don't really have any close friends here, yet. There's the woman I work with, but that's not the kind of thing you share with a co-worker." I paused, finally organizing my thoughts. "My sister. I told my sister."

"And what was her reaction?" Farrah asked.

"She was upset and supportive, of course, but we didn't really go into it too much."

Her brows pinched in the middle, casting a shadow over her eyes. "Why not?"

Again, I couldn't help but chuckle. "Why would I? She's got a lot going on in her life. The last thing I want to do is bother her with my stuff."

Unfolding her arms and rifling through the papers in my folder, Farrah pulled out some of her older notes. "When do you think you started believing you had to concede to other people's needs or wants before your own?"

Finally understanding where she was going, I deliberated on how honest to be. Eventually, I figured if I was paying for the hour, it couldn't hurt to be all in.

"I don't know. Maybe the first time I had to walk myself to school on a notoriously dangerous stretch of road when I was only six because my mom couldn't get out of bed." I shrugged. "Or maybe when I didn't want to lie to my parents but let my sister hide her cigarettes in my Easy-Bake Oven anyway, knowing I would get in serious trouble for it. I was willing to take those bullets if it helped the people I loved. It's just always been that way."

Farrah nodded, and I wondered for the first time if she had siblings. Maybe older parents who relied on her. I wondered if she understood where I came from because her training taught her to, or because she had once been in the same position.

"Here's what I'm going to suggest for the next week," Farrah scribbled a note on a piece of paper the way a doctor would write out a prescription. "First, when you're ready, I want you to reach back out to your sister and finish that conversation. It doesn't have to be long or deep or sad, but it's important that you start allowing yourself more closure and more support." She tapped the last line of her note with the end of her pen. "And secondly, I want you to focus entirely on your needs. Whether that is getting enough sleep, eating what makes you feel satisfied. Laughing, crying, screaming. What you need will come first."

It was such a beautiful notion, but I couldn't help laughing a little. "I'm so sorry, but I have kids, so that is not an option for me."

"Do you also have a husband?"

"Of course I do."

Slipping the paper into my hand, Farrah sat back. "Then I don't know why he can't offset some of the load while you work on offloading some of this trauma." She smiled that soft kind of smile she always had when she wanted to drive her point home. "A broken leg won't ever heal if you keep walking on it."

* * *

As a proud child of the workaholic generation, I would love to say that the week of putting myself first went off without a hitch. That I buckled down and dug into Farrah's assignment, allowing myself time to rest when I needed, play when I wanted, but that would be a complete crock of shit. In fact, it went embarrassingly poorly. And the embarrassing part was that I was the one who kept tripping up.

After coming home from my session with Farrah, I shared with Joe how I was supposed to be prioritizing myself. He immediately suggested I sleep in the next day and let him get the kids off to school before heading to work. The next day, I was up at 6 a.m.

A few nights later, trying to get back on track, I suggested that instead of cooking we order from a delicious Indian takeout place that I routinely dreamed about with its sweet butter chicken and spicy samosas. The kids, as children are wont to do when they hear the ingredients of something they aren't familiar, immediately protested. So, macaroni and cheese it was.

Joe tried his best, but the old saying "you can lead a horse to water, but you can't make it drink" is never truer than with someone who thinks their only value lies in their ability to be a good mother and wife. The one thing he did hold fast on was his plan to take me out to a special dinner for my birthday.

* * *

Holding the phone tightly against the side of my cheek, I counted my heartbeats in between the rings. The other half of Farrah's homework—to finish my conversation with my sister and find some sort of closure—was something I would have much rather stuck on the back burner and completely forgotten about. But whether because of that rare sisterly telepathic bond or simply a coincidence, Kami had reached out the morning of my birthday with well wishes and a request to call her later so we could talk.

Could I have put it off? Sure. That was one of the few pros of living so far away from your family. It's not like they can come bang down your door when you're avoiding issues. But avoidance was also the kind of behaviour that had driven a wedge into our relationship before, and that wasn't something I wanted to revisit.

On the fourth ring, Kami picked up. "Hey, kiddo. Happy birthday! What are you, eighty-nine now?"

I rolled my eyes, even though I knew she couldn't see the gesture. The younger sibling instinct never did go away. "Thirty-three, jerk face. I suppose, since you're seven years older than me, your memory must be going." I could hear her exaggerated scoffing across the line, and this return to playful banter felt nice. Like a glimpse into what used to be. But before I could rejoice in it too long, her tone changed, and I knew where the conversation was heading.

"I've been worried about you, kiddo." Her voice was soft, even with the rasp of a lifelong smoker. I could tell she was trying to be gentle. Coax me out of my shell.

My knee-jerk reaction was to turn inward, pretend like everything was hunky-dory and she had no need to worry about me. But even I—the person who had been orchestrating this façade of okay-ness—could see that it was getting harder and harder to maintain.

"I'm worried about me too."

There was a pause, then I heard her take a deep breath. "Are you talking to anyone? Does anyone else know?"

"Joe knows."

"Of course."

"I went to the hospital after it happened. They recommended a counsellor I've been seeing every week. It's definitely helping."

Another pause. Another deep breath.

"Have you told Mom? Or Dad?"

Kami and I had very different relationships with our parents, but both of us had always felt a sense of caretaking. Whether it had been walking on eggshells when the tension had become unbearable between them, even after the divorce, or shielding their feelings when one or the other offloaded their own trauma onto our shoulders in the form of strict parenting, we always felt as if we were walking a tightrope, never knowing whether, if we fell, they would catch us or scold us for falling.

"No, and I'm not really sure I want to." I sat on the edge of the bed and fiddled with the pocket of my jean jacket. Joe was still in the shower, but I had been ready hours ahead of our dinner date, knowing that as soon as we dropped the kids off with the sitter my anxiety would kick in.

"Can't say I blame you." I could hear a note of resentment in Kami's voice, and I wondered if there were skeletons in her closet she'd yet to share.

"I'm worried they'll think it's my fault. They don't know about the arrangement Joe and I have, and I can almost guarantee they won't understand it." I could feel a lump forming in my throat, an uncomfortable sadness left over from being a child who spent so much time alone, who very often felt unwanted or unloved. At the same time, it was a little refreshing to feel something other than fear or shame.

I was surprised when Kami laughed, a sharp, almost snarky laugh. "Oh no, kiddo. I can tell you this: They may not understand your arrangement with Joe, and they may be furious that the assault happened, but they will never think something like this is your fault."

"Really?" Even to my own ears, my voice sounded small, child-like. A whimper.

"I can promise you. And do you know why?" She paused, and when I didn't respond, she continued. "Because it's not. This is not your fault. Who gives a fuck if you have an open marriage or are full-blown swingers?"

Tears wet my cheeks before I even realized I was crying, and I choked out a half-sob, half-chuckle, "Polyamorous. Not open."

Kami made a *pfft* sound that vibrated across the line. "Whatever. The point is it doesn't matter if you had your husband's permission to be on that date or were running around behind his back or were completely single. What happened to you *was not your fault.*"

The tears were coming in streams now, the lump in my throat had swollen to an unimaginable size, and the only reply I could manage was a timid squeak of agreement. It was the first time I had acknowledged—both inwardly or outwardly—that the rape had not been my fault. And I prayed it was a notion I could keep hold of forever.

After an awkward few minutes of silence while I wiped my wet cheeks and snotty nose like a overtired toddler, we said our goodbyes and I tucked my cell phone into my purse. I wasn't sure how I was going to transition from that conversation to the jovial celebration of another journey around the sun, but part of me felt hopeful that this night might be the beginning of the next chapter.

* * *

Even before Farrah's assignment, Joe and I had tried to revive our date night traditions, but I found all of our old watering holes, or even new spots, either too loud, too busy, or too dark. All of the things that had initially attracted me to them, as a proud people watcher, were now the exact things that scared me away.

Then we found The Sociable House, just twenty minutes from home. Its name was derived from a popular maritime drinking game—Sociables. The game was built on a very loose set of rules and involved a deck of cards and a lot of alcohol. Which meant that by the end of the game either everyone was in love or in a fight. Usually the latter.

The little pub immediately endeared itself to me: every wall adorned with crooked paintings of tilted sailing ships, the bar swathed in rich cedar and oak, the sound of good conversation and good music, the smell of freshly smoked fish. And it was all run by a welcoming maritime couple who, like Joe and me, had moved their families from the East Coast in search of more opportunities. It was a place of comfort, a place that felt like home in a time when I felt completely unmoored. It was the perfect place to celebrate anything, especially my birthday.

Joe sat across from me on a stool at one of the high-top tables— the kind that, if you were like me and not blessed with legs longer than your arms, you had to sort of hop on and scoot back into. I always felt like an overgrown child at those tables, my feet swinging below me and well above the floor. But this one did give me a good view of the rest of the room.

Much like a weathered hitman in a Bruce Willis action flick, I'd started choosing my seating not based on proximity to the bar

or band or bathroom. Instead, my back had to face the wall. Just
the thought of someone being able to approach me from behind
sent shivers creeping across my skin. But that night, even though
I'd chosen the position out of habit, the reason had barely crossed
my mind. The soft lighting of the pub and the three glasses of red
wine I'd enjoyed made it easy to fall into a sort of swoon when the
conversation died down, and I sat there watching Joe.

Even in the dark, his blue eyes were still bright and the wisps
of silver that had begun to show in his beard continued to catch my
attention. He was an attractive guy when we'd first met, but now
he'd grown into this handsome man. Looking at him made it easy
to let my guard down. Just a little. Just for the night.

"Hello?" Joe called over the hum of other voices, letting the
word drag out in exaggeration. "Am I boring you?" I knew he was
teasing by the way his eyes pinched at the corners, the creases only
giving him a more distinguished look.

"No, no, sorry. I was just admiring you, actually." I reached across
the table and threaded my fingers through his. PDA had been
few and far between since the attack, but just lately, I found that
if I initiated them, they could be sweetly reassuring. They were a
reminder that Joe, and our relationship, was the real, tangible thing
in the ongoing nightmare of my life.

"Oh, I'm sure you were." His bushy brow, ever a source of frustration for my grooming obsession, arched as he cast a glance over
his shoulder. "You sure you weren't checking out the bartender? I
know he's your type."

Behind the bar stood the human equivalent of an oak tree. All
thickness and strength. Joe was right. I liked a man who looked like
he could withstand a hurricane, but instead of denying it, I decided
to lean into the game.

"Maybe." I let my eyes wander over the floor and stop at a nearby
table. "Or maybe I was actually admiring our server."

A short, curvy brunette flitted from table to table, effortlessly
depositing drinks and scooping up stacks of plates. I wasn't sure if

it was how calm she was in the calamity of service or the warmth of her smile that had grabbed my attention from the moment we walked in, but something had. And for a moment, I allowed myself to enjoy it. Even though I'd been the one to press pause on non-monogamy, I still missed the dynamic.

"Well, you can't have both. That's just not fair." Joe quietly pounded his fists on the table, pretending to throw a toddler-level fit. I couldn't help but laugh, remembering how it used to feel when this was the norm. The playful banter, the ease of expression. The few people we had been open with about our marriage could never see the motivation, assuming it was always about the sex. But it was this, the deep and non-judgemental understanding of the other. Who they were, what they wanted, what they needed to be happy. This was why we did it.

There was a time when things had been so bad—Joe on the couch and me curled up alone in our bed—times when I'd thought it was over and we'd never recover. But those times made sitting here with him now, comfortable and safe, all the more special.

My laughter was cut short and we both clammed up, like two kids getting caught swearing in class, as our waitress brought another round of drinks and an order of steamed mussels to the table. I soaked in the buttery aroma while Joe added pepper and lemon to the mix. Plucking a shell from the bowl, I used my fork to scoop out the meat and dip it in the butter mixture before popping it in my mouth. If home could be a flavour, this may have very well been it.

The wine had finally made its way through me and the bathroom called my name. Hopping down off the stool, I gave Joe a playful look of warning.

"At least half of those better still be there when I get back." I gave his arm a squeeze and made my way through the crowd.

As in most establishments of this vintage, the bathrooms here were clearly an after-thought—tucked away down a dimly lit stairway, sharing an equally dark hallway with a handful of storage closets. To my surprise, I had made it all the way down, into the stall, had finished my business, and was washing my hands at the sink before my brain even acknowledged the minefield of creepy corners I had just navigated. And it might never have switched on the warning siren if I hadn't caught a whiff of his cologne.

Letting the warm water run over my hands, I barely noticed the woman at the sink next to me until she left, swinging the door open and letting it close slowly behind her. The muffled sounds of shuffling feet and raised voices above me filtered in through the gradually closing gap, which I would have expected. What I didn't expect was the sickly sweet smell of citrus, nearly smothered by an aggressive hit of mint and odd undertones of some unknown woodsy scent. It wafted in through the opening—no, it *rushed* in and sucker-punched me in the gut. It was the exact same cheap drugstore cologne Liam had been wearing the night he raped me.

Hurrying to the door, I pressed my back against the wall beside it and counted the beats as my heart drummed in my chest. This was beyond an overreaction. Some young dishwasher had likely just wandered down the hall to sneak outside for his fifth smoke of the night, and I'd gotten caught in his downdraft.

If Farrah had been there, she would have reminded me of how real traumatic memories could feel, and that my mind was simply being triggered as a response to the scent and everything it brought to mind. That there was no danger. That I did not have to flee. Only problem was, Farrah wasn't there. No one was. I was all alone in that room, my mind bursting at its seams with fear. There was no space left for rational thinking.

After checking my pockets and realizing I'd left my cell phone at the table with Joe, I knew I had no option but to make my way back to the table. Inhaling deeply and holding that breath safely in my chest, I flung open the bathroom door, scanned the hall, and bolted for the stairs. Taking them two at a time, I stopped abruptly at the top, teetering on the edge of the landing. The rest of the patrons were continuing their evenings as if nothing nefarious was happening, and no monster was lurking in their midst. Immediately, my fear was pushed aside to make room for embarrassment. My brain couldn't decide whether it should protect me or be ashamed of me.

Clenching my hands into fists and letting my nails dig into the soft flesh of my palms—a trick I'd taught myself for when the urge to hyperventilate started to rise—I moved quickly across the room. Head down, eyes focusing only on the back of Joe's shirt. Once I made it, I snatched the strap of my purse from the hook behind our table and grabbed Joe's hand.

Leaning in, I whispered in his ear, "We have to go."

He pulled away, rocking back to look at my face. "What are you talking about? We haven't even finished dinner."

I squeezed his hand, hard. "I have to go. Now. I can't do this. I'm sorry."

Releasing his grip, I made a beeline for the front door, accidentally hip-checking the beautiful brunette server as I passed. Muttering mortified apologies, I continued my trajectory until I swung through the door and felt the cold winter air snap against my face. I stopped when my feet hit the pavement of the parking lot. A wave of nausea slammed into the back of my throat, causing me to double over. Hands on my knees, my head swinging between my shoulders, I fought off the inevitable panic attack. This time with a possible side helping of public vomiting.

"What the fuck, Eden? Are you okay?" Joe jogged over, struggling to shove his wallet back into his pants pocket, holding my cell phone and purse in his other hand. He'd probably left a wad of cash on the table in a hurry to follow me. I'd probably embarrassed him terribly. But in yet another wildly irrational shift of emotions, I could no longer feel the shame I had earlier, or the fear. Instead, a hot needle-prick of anger scratched at the back of my head. Begging to be let out.

Joe folded at the waist and placed his hand on my shoulder in an attempt to comfort me. It did the exact opposite.

Snapping upright, I flung his hand off and snatched my belongings from his grasp. "Don't fucking touch me! Why does everyone have to fucking touch me all the time?"

Joe held his hands aloft, but took a step closer. "Okay, I won't touch you. But please tell me what's going on. Did something happen when you went to the bathrooms? This isn't like you."

I raked my hands through my hair, pulling at the ends to feel something other than this anger. "Of course it's not! Nothing I do anymore is 'like me.' Who the fuck am I anymore? I can't leave the house without a chaperone. I'm terrified of the dark, like some stupid baby. I don't sleep, I don't eat, I don't laugh, I don't fuck. I had to change my goddamn phone number, just so he wouldn't be able to harass me anymore!"

Even in the dark parking lot, lit only by sporadic pools of streetlights, I could see the shift in Joe's expression.

"What do you mean he's harassing you? Who?" He had drawn out each word, slow and clear, clinging to control.

And just like that, the anger retreated and I couldn't find my volume. "The guy who…"

"Him? He's been messaging you? Calling you? Saying what?"

I picked at an imaginary hangnail, unable to meet Joe's eyes. I hadn't lied, but I had withheld, knowing how badly it would hurt him if he knew the things I'd been dealing with. And yet here he was, his heart breaking all over the dusty pavement of a dark parking lot. It seemed I wasn't the only one I couldn't protect.

"It doesn't matter anymore. That's why I changed my number— and he hasn't contacted me since. I think he finally got the hint." I stepped toward him, my hands searching for his. "I'm really sorry. Telling you just seemed like an unnecessary burden, especially since you've already got enough on your plate. I figured I could handle it myself."

Joe shrugged off my touch. "I think it's obvious you can't handle any of this by yourself." He moved around me, stomping toward the car. Punching a button on his key fob, he waited while the trunk hatch popped open and then started to rummage through it.

"I said I was sorry. It's not exactly like I know how to handle something like this!" I made my way across the parking lot and pulled open the passenger-side door.

"Yeah, well I do." Slamming the trunk lid closed, Joe swung a silver baseball bat over his shoulder and strode to the driver's side.

"No, no, no." Running around the front of the car, I reached up and tugged the bat down. We held it between us in a tense tug of war. "That won't fix anything, Joe. You know that. Plus, how would you even find him?"

He tightened his grip on the weapon. "He found you."

There was a venom in his voice that scared me. The kind of tone that told me he could easily become another kind of monster, if it kept me safe. But it was his eyes, glassy and wet beneath his pinched brows, that betrayed his bravado and revealed the sadness he was hiding.

"It won't happen again, I promise." I gave one last tug and pulled the bat free of his hand.

"You can't promise that"—he choked on a sob that threatened to escape—"and neither can I."

He wasn't wrong. I searched his face for some sign that he knew what to do next; he was always the planner, the problem solver. Many times in our early years, when the only thing we could afford was bread, butter, and milk, he would be the one to hold me tight and assure me that we'd get through it together. But I didn't see that determination now, only the loss of hope.

"What if I speak to a detective?" I looked away, focusing instead on the weight of the bat in my hand. "My counsellor said they could bring in someone for me to talk to. Not like a formal report, but just so I could understand the process better if I did want to eventually."

A static-filled pause passed before I felt Joe's arms wrap around me, pulling me into his chest. My cheek pressed against his cotton T-shirt, cool after standing in the cold November night air, and his chin rested atop my head.

"Thank you."

For the first time in months, I felt like I'd maybe done something right. Taken back even the tiniest amount of control over this downward spiral my life had seemingly nosedived into. And, in turn, chipped away some of the burden Joe had been carrying. Both sensations felt good. It wasn't the chapter I had envisioned entering earlier in the night, but it was forward momentum none the less.

CHAPTER 8

Detective
No Justice

A BLACK COFFEE SAT BEFORE ME IN A PAPER CUP. I'D PASSED ON THE powdered creamer when Farrah offered it, but as I took a sip of the bitter brew, I wished I'd just opted for water instead. But the aroma alone gave me the feeling of planting my feet firmly on the ground. A familiar comfort. And right now, sitting in the same office where Farrah conducted our therapy sessions, waiting for a detective from the sexual crimes unit, I needed all the comfort I could muster.

After my meltdown at Sociables, I'd asked Farrah if I could speak with someone about the options I had if I were to pursue criminal charges. It took several weeks for her to arrange an appointment that fit everyone's schedule, which gave me more than enough time to cancel and rebook the session repeatedly.

Justice is one of those fickle things that everyone wants and so few receive—to the point where you start wondering whether the hype is real. Other than putting him behind bars and ensuring he could never hurt me again, what would the end result be?

Would I be heralded as a hero? Someone who had stood for what was right and just, putting a stop to the inhumane treatment of women's bodies?

Part of me wanted to believe that as much as I wanted to believe fairies were real and I could buy a timeshare in Neverland. And that part of me kept my butt planted firmly in the stiff plastic chair inside Farrah's office, waiting to meet the person who would either crush or cultivate that fantasy.

When the office door cracked open, there was no tall brooding detective immediately entering the room, just like in the movies. Instead, a woman in a neat black blazer with dark hair pulled back into a severe ponytail sauntered in. Reaching across the table, she extended her hand. "Detective McKinnon."

I took her hand, a firm handshake. Two pumps. Neat and to the point.

Farrah stood near the door. "Would you like me to stay?" Her fingers were knitted together, and I could tell she was nervous for me.

"No, it's okay." I tried to summon a smile. "But thank you."

As the door closed and Farrah left, the air in the room suddenly felt stale. I took another sip of the coffee; it was cold now, adding an extra bite to the bitterness.

Detective McKinnon leaned forward in the chair opposite me, her hands clasped in front of her. "Dr. Bhole tells me you asked to speak with a detective."

I nodded and took another sip.

"So you are aware I have been working with the centre for a while now, as well as twenty-five years on the SVU. While this isn't a formal statement, you can tell me in as much or as little detail why you wanted to speak with me today. As per patient confidentiality, Dr. Bhole didn't explain the reason for our chat. Would you like to?"

"No, but that would probably be a waste of your time."

I chuckled. She didn't.

I cleared my throat, averting my eyes from her intense gaze, and stared into the inky blackness inside my cup. "I was raped."

There was a small, sharp inhale, and I heard the back of her chair softly creaking. Looking up I saw Detective McKinnon was now leaning back, her arms crossed over her chest. Funnily enough, the posture reminded me of my father. His thick arms, freckled with dark spots from too many summers in the Atlantic sun, folded neatly atop his round belly, leaning back in his chair the way he always did when he knew whatever story we were excitedly telling would be a long one. Another odd comfort in a deeply uncomfortable environment.

"Would you like to go into more detail?"

Would I? Of course. Did I want to? Absolutely not. I was pretty sure another joke about my reluctancy to cooperate wouldn't fly, and the long legs under her crisp black dress pants told me she could outrun me if I decided to bolt, so there were no other options than to just start at the beginning.

As I went through the details about where he touched and pinched and bit, Detective McKinnon sat perfectly still. She didn't give off the same nurturing feeling as the nurse from my hospital visit, or the empathy of Farrah. She was more detached, more calculating. Even her resemblance to my father's mannerisms had started to frost over. I couldn't tell if she was scrutinizing every word that I spoke to find any flaw in the recounting, but by the time I had finished I could feel the puddle of black coffee in my belly beginning to spoil.

Tilting the paper cup back against my lips, I let the last few drops wet my mouth while I waited for her response.

Leaning forward, Detective McKinnon propped both elbows on the desk between us, steepled her fingers, and pressed them against her lips before speaking.

"What happened to you, Ms. Boudreau was horrific, and should never have happened."

"Mrs." I corrected, unsure why it mattered. But it mattered.

Pausing to process the momentary interruption and deem it unimportant, she calmly, and with little emotion, continued. "From what you've told me, I gather the man who attacked you knew exactly what he was doing. He had planned it out, and nothing you could have done would have changed the trajectory of that night."

I could feel the bitter coffee in my stomach attempting to make its way back up.

"Which makes me think he has probably done this before, and won't hesitate to do it again." She leaned in closer, just a hint of strain in the corners of her eyes. "You really should consider reporting, Mrs. Boudreau."

I wasn't some naive college co-ed who thought "boys will be boys" was a reasonable excuse for the routine sexual violence that women around the world were subjected to. I watched the news, read the books and *The New York Times* articles, followed the hashtags. But the reality of a seasoned detective, one who had likely seen the worst of the worst, confirming fears I hadn't even realized yet—that he had done this to other women, and that not reporting might allow him to do it to someone else—slammed against my chest like a sledgehammer.

"But I want you to know exactly what you are getting yourself into if you do." Detective McKinnon tapped on the desk with one subtly manicured finger. "If you choose to report, you can't just walk into any station. You'll have to figure out which is in the boundaries of where the assault occurred."

A bubble of stomach acid rose to the back of my throat, forcing an audible gulping as I struggled to steady my breath.

"Once you've arrived at the correct station, you will have to be prepared that you could get stuck with an officer who is just getting off a long shift." Detective McKinnon punctuated her words by tapping even harder on the desktop. "One who is tired and cranky and has no patience for filling out paperwork. They won't make it easy. They're not there to hold your hand or give you a shoulder to cry on. They want the facts and only the facts."

I shifted my weight and tried to plant my feet firmly on the floor. The room was starting to tilt.

"After they take your report, they will decide whether or not there is enough evidence to even press charges." She paused to consider that. "Since you did the rape kit and the medical file would have your statement of the assault documented, there would likely be enough."

Squeezing the paper cup in my hand, I tried to focus on the sound of it crumbling in my palm. Her words were landing like punches to the gut, and I wasn't sure how many more I could take.

"Although to press charges, they have to find him. You said you have a first name and a phone number?"

I thought about all the unknown numbers in my call list. "Yes, but I'm not sure if the number he gave me was really his."

Detective McKinnon sat back, propping her ankle up on her knee, "That could be an issue." She clicked her tongue against the roof of her mouth. "Well, let's just assume they can manage to trace him via the number, locate him and press charges. It would then be up to the courts to decide whether or not it should even go to trial. If they do, it could be anywhere from two to five years before you see the inside of a courtroom, and in that time, his defence team would be building their case. Which would entail scrutinizing every aspect of your story and"—she paused—"lifestyle."

The room titled a little further.

I'd always known this would be a sticking point. When Joe and I first chose to explore an open marriage, we'd kept it private, for the most part. Only our closest friends knew about the arrangement, and even they thought we were out of our minds. Most people would rather dig their heels into a bad marriage than consider anything other than divorce to mend what was broken.

Yes, it wasn't a traditional relationship, but did that invalidate my right to basic safety? Consent? Human decency?

"If you do go to court"—she leaned forward and placed her hands on the table—"and this is the part I hate telling people, but it's important to know, there is only a four percent chance you would get a conviction." Pausing, Detective McKinnon searched my face as if she trying to determine if that statistic was truly sinking in. When I didn't flinch or reply or even breath, she repeated. "Four percent."

It took several seconds longer than it should have to register in my mind. Farrah would later say it was shock, but I think my brain simply shutdown like a computer infected with a nasty virus. When it came back online, my first reaction was one even I couldn't have predicted. I laughed. I laughed so hard I had to hold my sides. When I managed to regain my composure, Detective McKinnon's curious stare had not budged. Guess she'd seen this before.

"So what you're really saying is there is only a four percent chance they will believe me?" Now I leaned across the table, letting my arms rest just a hair from hers. "If, and only if I can jump through every flaming hoop they hold up for me, change their minds on why 'non-monogamy' does not equal 'sex worker with no right to consent,' and put myself and my family through hell for up to five years—then *maybe* there is a four percent chance I will get justice?"

For the first time since Detective McKinnon had entered the room, I saw something other than intensity cloud her features. Pity.

I'm not sure if it was that look or the grim play-by-play that had preceded it, but in that moment something inside me broke. Not shattered or splintered, but snapped clean in half. As if the very last fragment of my former self that had been holding me together had finally been severed.

"It may seem that way, but it's not hopeless. You should still consider reporting."

Numb, I nodded.

We both knew I wouldn't.

As she stood to leave, straightening her suit jacket, she pulled a business card from her pocket and placed it in front of me on the desk. "In case you change your mind."

Opening the door to leave, she turned back one last time and said something that implanted itself under my skin like a prickly thorn. One I would likely never be able to remove. "You know, if it had to happen to anyone, I'm glad it happened to someone as strong as you."

Rationally, I knew it was meant to be inspiring, a compliment, but it felt like bullshit. What was the point of being strong? So I could carry around this trauma for the rest of my life? Along with the heavy weight of shame because the people put in positions to protect me wouldn't believe me? I didn't believe I was strong enough for that, and I didn't know if I wanted to be.

After the detective left, Farrah took her place in the doorway, her hands still clasped together, worry etching lines into her young face.

"Are you okay?" she asked.

Turning in my chair, I was ready to scoff and make some sarcastic remark. Pretend the meeting had gone as horribly as I'd assumed it would and suggest we just go back to our regularly scheduled keep-Eden-from-going-off-the-deep-end sessions. But then the floor fell out from below me.

I dropped to my knees on the hard carpeted floor, gagging into my palm and reaching for the waste basket. Farrah rushed to tuck it under my chin as the contents of my stomach came rushing up. The remnants of bitter coffee burned my throat and salty tears stung my eyes.

"It's okay. Take a deep breath. It's going to be okay." Farrah rubbed my back in soft circles, only stopping to pull a damp strand of hair off my forehead.

Up until that point, I had trusted Farrah with every ounce of faith I had left. Knew, without a doubt, that she would never sugarcoat the truth. But in that moment, she lied to me for the first and last time.

CHAPTER 9

Fine Lines

AFTER I INTENTIONALLY MISSED MY NEXT THREE APPOINTMENTS with Farrah, she stopped calling to reschedule. Part of me was relieved when the missed call notifications came to an end, but another part was a little disappointed. Maybe she knew I needed space. Or maybe I'd just successfully pushed her away. It was a go-to personality trait of mine when things got really rough.

It was a lot easier to isolate myself now that it felt like I was walking through a thick, muted fog. The bright lights of the Christmas decorations that had gone up everywhere since I met with the detective, the joy of my sons during what should have been a festive season, Joe's persistent attempts at positivity—none of it could penetrate the fog. The only things that did seem to occasionally make their way through were the intrusive thoughts that had taken up residency in the back of my mind.

Why should anyone believe me? It's his word against mine. He's innocent until proven guilty, right? So why do I feel like I'm guilty of being a lying whore until proven innocent? Probably because I've been raised to believe my bra straps and exposed skin and general feminine presence can cause men of all ages to succumb to their uncontrollable lust. Apparently, the justice system also runs on the "Boys will be boys" theory.

When the fog couldn't keep the thoughts away, whiskey stepped in to help. Soon enough, though, drinking by myself at home started to get old—and as much as I wanted to return to the comfort of The Sociable House, going there to drown my sorrows in bottomless whiskeys felt like blasphemy. Which was why, instead, I started frequenting a local dive bar, Lakesides, with an old friend, John.

* * *

It was New Year's Eve eve—and everyone seemed ready to bid 2017 farewell and welcome in 2018. I, on the other hand, didn't give two shits. You'd think I would have been the first one in line to flip off the past year and move into the next, but I had adopted a new sense of apathy that made it nearly impossible to get on the celebration train.

The flashing blue neon lights did nothing to detract from the sticky spilled substance that coated the bar top. I chuckled into my nearly empty glass when I thought about how, not so long ago, the creak of wind passing through a branch or a whiff of the wrong cologne would have sent me into hiding like a shivering, scared pup. Now I was sitting shoulder-to-shoulder with strange men reeking of booze and cigarettes as their leering eyes roamed over me without shame.

As I pressed the glass to my lips and let the spicy amber liquid burn my throat on its way down, all I could think was: *Turns out warm whiskey and a lack of hope help to wash away a fear of men a lot faster than therapy.*

That attitude, no matter how foolish in hindsight, was likely why I hadn't seen Farrah at all since my meeting with Detective McKinnon. What was the point? Fix my head just so I can live with the knowledge that the man who violated and threatened me would almost surely continue to walk around free, never being punished for what he'd done? Seemed like a waste of time and money to me.

A hand on my shoulder caused me to jump, and I cursed the instinctual reflexes even drinking couldn't do away with.

"Can you hurry up and finish your drink? I want to go out for a smoke." John purred into my ear.

John was an old friend. Friend with benefits. Except this time, the only benefits were that he never asked if I'd had too much to drink. In fact, he was the first to order another round. He was a good time, and our relationship had never been deep. Which was exactly what I needed, and exactly what made Joe worry about my reunion with him.

At first, Joe had been happy to see me getting out of the house. My hermit ways had amplified since my meeting with the detective. No morning runs, no trips to the library or bookstore, and certainly no intimacy. Eventually, my patience became paper thin, and picking fights had become my new nightly tradition. Joe insisted the drinking wasn't helping it, and I insisted he keep his opinions to himself.

Truth was, I knew I was taking the easy way out. Avoiding my fears and issues by pouring another glass. One shot turns into two, which turns into four, which turns into half a pack of cigarettes and a handful of Tylenol to ward off the impending hangover.

"Okay, jeez." I tilted my head back and swallowed the last mouthful of my drink, letting the remnants of ice skip over each other when I slid the empty glass across the bar.

I cursed under my breath, struggling to shove my arms into the thick winter coat I'd finally had to dig out of the storage closet earlier that week. John held the door open, the chunky black logo for Lakesides on the glass obscuring my view of the parking lot slightly. When I stepped out into an ankle-high drift of snow, a tiny gasp of surprise eked its way out.

John chuckled and tucked his mousey brown hair into the folds of his hood. "They said we were supposed to get a few centimetres tonight."

I kicked at the offensive white fluff. "Yeah, but that wasn't supposed to start until, like, eleven."

He paused in the middle of pulling a cigarette from his pack and just stared at me. "It's one.

"Shut up." I fumbled to find which pocket I'd stuffed my cell phone in, finally pulling it out and holding it close to my face so the screen would stop shaking the way it liked to after a I'd had a few too many. "Shit, I was supposed to be home at midnight." I typed out a quick text message to Joe letting him know I was okay, time had gotten away from me, and I'd be home in the next hour. I only partially believed my own bullshit.

I was almost positive Joe wouldn't be waiting up. In the first little while after the assault, he had been on almost as high an alert as I had, worried when I was even five minutes late getting home from dropping the kids off or not answering my phone while grocery shopping. But now, the distance between us had tripled—if not quadrupled—and he'd finally stopped asking about my comings and goings. Maybe he still worried, but that wasn't something I could think about because then I would feel guilty that I didn't.

I shoved the phone back into my pocket and started another search, this time for my bottle of Tylenol.

"What the hell are you digging for in there?" John hooked the lip of my purse and tugged it toward him. I snatched it back, shooting him a snarky look. It was hard to stay irritated with him though, what with his big brown eyes and that boyish grin that let you know he regularly talked himself out of trouble.

Holding up an empty bottle and shaking it, I groaned. "I've got a splitting headache. No more drinking for me, I guess."

I chucked the bottle into a nearby trash can. John shuffled up beside me. Even through the thick fabric of my coat, I could feel the warmth of his arm against mine. It should have made me uncomfortable. We hadn't revived the benefits portion of our friendship, and, frankly, I had no intentions of doing so. But his touch didn't frustrate or excite me. It was just another invasion of my space I was forced to accept. Complain and I was a cold bitch. Playfully deflect and I was leading him on. Damned if you do, damned if you don't.

Just then, a group of men stumbled out of the bar, yelling loudly and roughhousing with each other. Without warning, a wave of automated responses to that trigger caused every muscle in my body to stiffen and my breath to catch in my lungs. I backed up until my rear bumped up against the side of my car, and I held my bag in front of me defensively.

I could tell John had noticed the shift in my mood, but neither of us wanted to acknowledge it. In an attempt to distract me, John leaned down and, with his mouth just inches from my ear and his hot breath warming my cheek, said, "We don't have to call it a night just yet. I have something different that will help with the headache." I knew he wasn't talking about ibuprofen or a soothing peppermint oil, but the idea of going home didn't appeal to me quite yet, so I nodded and followed him back inside.

We slung our coats haphazardly over two stools at the bar, and then John led us toward the washrooms. They were nestled in the far back corner of the bar, beyond a small alcove of empty pool tables. To call them washrooms was generous—supply closets with a sink and a toilet was more accurate. But they were just big enough for John to pull me into one and silently lock the door behind us.

Once he was sure we weren't going to be interrupted, John reached into his wallet and pulled out a small, clear baggy that had been tucked in between a coffee stamp card and a stack of crumpled receipts. When he shook it, a grin I didn't love crept across his face. In a clearly well-practiced motion, he used his credit card to arrange five neat white lines of the powder on the counter. After he'd finished, he retrieved a crumpled twenty-dollar bill from his pocket and rolled it into a perfect tube. Without a word, he held out the rolled-up bill for me to take.

Part of me wanted to be offended that he'd assumed I would know what to do with the money he handed me. This wasn't an activity we had ever tried together. But another, snarkier part reminded me that this wasn't exactly my first time. Just my first time in a long time.

You'd think having such a prominent example of addiction in my early years would have guaranteed I'd stay far away from illicit activities, but in my early twenties I'd wanted to blur the lines between real life and nightlife just as much as the next person. When you're young and invincible, it's easy to dabble in powder and pills, wake up the next day with a bottle of water and a Red Bull, and carry on with life. It was even easier when I set myself a strict code of conduct: never from my sister's stash, or with her. If I was going to be a bad influence, it wouldn't be on her. If I had to pay for it, I wouldn't want it. If whoever was throwing the house party or footing the bill for the VIP room offered, I was more than happy to imbibe. But it was never allowed to become something I needed. It was something to keep me awake, to keep the party going. At that time, it was nothing like the addiction that had gained a foothold in my family, and as long as I could see that clear demarcation, then I was still in control and could stop anytime I wanted.

What's funny about youth is the lack of perspective. The only reason I maintained control in my younger years was my motivation. Then, I just wanted to have a good time. Let loose and act my age for once, toss away the responsibility I carried for everyone and be just a little reckless. But now, standing over a counter in a dingy bar with bad decisions nibbling on my earlobes, begging me to indulge for just a moment, my motivation was wildly different.

I didn't want to have a good time; I wanted to do something other than simply exist. I'd started to feel like the single streetlight that had lit the parking lot where I was assaulted. It stood sentry but also forgotten. An assumed staple of the landscape with its patinaed metal dinged and scratched, its bulb flickering and holding on to its light for just one more evening. It was there, but only in the periphery, which was exactly how I felt. And I didn't want to feel that way anymore. So I held that crisp green bill tightly between my fingers, bent down, inhaled, and let the strangely satisfying burn ignite whatever was left inside me.

* * *

There's a phenomenon called lucid dreaming. I can't remember where I first learned about it. Maybe on some late night Nat Geo channel rerun. Who knows. It's a state of slumber in which the dreamer is completely asleep but also completely aware that they are dreaming. An awareness of their unawareness, you could say.

Sometimes, the dreamer can gain a minute amount of control over the figures, narratives, or surroundings in the dream. But more often than not, they fall into a state of continually reaching for reality and watching it slip between their fingers like sand, over and over.

When the cocaine burns its way through my body and sinks its claws deep into my nervous system, I imagine that what I'm feeling is not so different from what those lucid dreamers feel. You are still yourself—a transparent, slippery version of yourself who does whatever she wants, believing there will be no consequences or regrets. It's as if you suddenly become aware of the hundreds of watts of electricity that skip back and forth between your synapses like children on a playground with a jumping rope. Every cell in my body had been on constant high alert since the moment I'd fled that dark parking lot, but when I did line after line, they seemed to find new purpose. They jittered and spun, bouncing around under my skin, small orbs of energy I could channel into anything I wanted—not just fear.

In reality, I was completely out of control. I'd gone from hiding in the shadows to dancing on bar stools. From sleeping for hours on end and finding solace under the covers to staying awake for days in a vain attempt to balance my precarious partying with my home life. But in my mind, the only time I was in control was when I was high. I could be funny, flirtatious, fearless. The options of emotions to choose from were endless, and I could choose, for the first time in months, to not be afraid. The only flaw in what I saw as a flawless plan was that eventually every well dries up. And it dries up even faster when you're drinking from it as if you'd rather drown than stop to take a breath.

* * *

A few weeks later, I was riding in John's car with the window down, my hair blowing in the bitter wind and my mind following at a terrifying clip. Looking over at the speedometer, glowing red in the dark night, I watched as the needle climbed until it sputtered at nearly 200 kilometres an hour. My brain wondered if I should be afraid. If I should tell him to slow down. Demand he get off the highway and take the backroads home. But I didn't.

Suddenly, lights appeared over the crest of the next hill, coming straight toward us. John slammed his foot into the brake, slowing us to an acceptable speed as they passed. But as soon as we could no longer see tail lights in the mirror, he took off again. It was a game he—well, we, because I never declined his invitation to come for a ride—had started to play when Lakesides had gotten too boring and the coke kept us awake long after last call.

This little game of chicken did nothing for me, though I assumed John thought it did. His hands had started creeping closer and closer to my skin as the speedometer topped out. This was another game we'd been playing: cat-and-mouse. Before, when I was still confidently expanding my sexual appetite, it was a game I would have excitedly taken part in. Now it did nothing but irritate me.

As John's hand attempted to roam from the stick shift to my knee again, I shifted in my seat, turning my knees toward the door and angling my legs out of his reach. Over the loud thrum of bass from his car speakers I heard him chuckle, which only irritated me more. Finally finished with his game, John pulled off the highway and wove his way through the side streets of some town I wasn't familiar with before pulling into the gravel lot of a dark park.

Turning off the engine but leaving the battery on, John changed the music to something softer. Raspy, soulful voices, melodic and almost romantic. A long-dormant feeling fluttered inside my stomach. I couldn't quite define it at first, but then, as the acoustic guitar strummed, I realized what it was—longing. Not longing for just anyone or anything. And not just for the before times, either. It was a longing for something much more specific. For intimacy. For that closeness, the bond of two people who have complete trust in each other. Who will give all of themselves and receive all in return. The small flutter turned into a swelling ache.

Pulling me from my thoughts was John's hand, yet again roaming over my leg. Jerking away, I reached into the centre console and pulled out one of the clear plastic baggies he kept there. I grabbed a bill from my jacket pocket and started rolling it. I was hoping to shift John's attention from my body to another bump. And, if I was lucky, to quiet the growing need in my belly.

After a few more lines and several more attempts to get his hands on me, it was clear that John wasn't getting the message I'd subtly been trying to send.

"Keep your hands to your fucking self! Jesus." I pushed away his hand and slammed my fist into the door, scrambling to find the handle.

"Oh, stop playing," he said as he reached for me again. This time, though, all of the pent-up frustration and resentment I'd been carrying for the past few months propelled me into motion. I threw open the car door and stomped across the parking lot. Leaning against the side of a rickety picnic table, I tried to catch my breath.

I could hear John yelling from the car to get back in, but I ignored him. A few moments later, the car engine revved to life and the tires kicked up small rocks and dust as John swung the car around so that his window was facing me. With one arm slung lazily out the window and a grin from ear to grin, John looked me in the eyes and said, "You used to be such a little freak."

"You're a little freak."

The same words Liam had said to me just moments after he'd shoved his fist inside me because his limp dick wouldn't cooperate. The same words men had used to degrade me when I turned down their advances, and that women used to shame me when I was open about my sexuality.

I snapped.

"I used to be a lot of fucking things. But I'm pretty sure being a freak doesn't automatically give you the go-ahead to let your dirty hands crawl all over me. It doesn't give you carte blanche to fondle me or fuck me. Whether I'm a freak or a slut or a whore or a saint, you don't have any right to fucking touch me."

His dark eyes grew wide and he muttered under his breath, "This bitch is crazy..."

"Of course I am! My head is on a constant swivel. High alert, all the time. It feels like there are live wires inside me."

For a moment, I thought he was going to ask me why. Ask what had happened to make me this way. But it was just a moment, and in the next second that glimmer of curiosity passed. His tone was cold and, with both hands on the wheel, he barked at me to get in the car so he could drive me home. Hesitantly, I climbed in, and as John sped back on to the road, without even thinking, I reached for the small baggie again. My fingers trembled as I held it. The fine layer of white powder seemed to call to me, like a craving. Before I could regret what would come next, I dropped it back into the console and turned to stare out the window, feeling incredibly raw. It was almost worse than feeling nothing at all.

I didn't pause outside the door when John dropped me off at home. Didn't bother to gain my composure. Just stormed inside and threw myself into the shower. It felt as if my self-awareness had been in hibernation, or maybe just hiding, but was now more present than ever. As I scrubbed at my skin, it felt hopeless that I could wash away the disgust and hatred I felt for how far I'd let myself fall. And how much further I was afraid I might go.

After I'd let the water run cold, I wrapped a towel around my wet body and padded softly toward the bedroom. The light from the bathroom spilled into the hallway and drifted into the room, landing on Joe, who was fast asleep beneath the sheets. For the first time in months, I took notice of his body, the way it curved under the sheets. The longing I'd felt in the car began to stir again, swelling into an insatiable ache. That's when I realized the longing hadn't just been for intimacy, that it had been for him—for Joe. And I wondered if I could just have a taste of how things used to be. I wondered if, just maybe, I could claw my way out of the hole I'd dug myself into.

Climbing beneath the sheets with Joe, I let my fingertip trace an invisible trail over his skin, from freckle to freckle. He groaned and began to stir. For a moment, I considered stopping. Rolling over and letting him think he had been dreaming. But I couldn't ignore that ache any longer. The truth hit me like a ton of bricks—I missed sex. I missed the intimacy, the anticipation, the pleasure. And I wanted to be brave enough to take it back.

Letting my hands return to their wandering, I soaked in the sounds of enjoyment that came from his chest as his moans grew deeper, more primal, more urgent. Each groan told me how much he enjoyed my touch, and I enjoyed that he enjoyed it, so I went a step further. Or lower. When Joe's mind finally caught up with his body, his eyes fluttered open and he struggled to focus on my face in the dark. Reaching down, he held my hand still for just a moment.

"Are you sure you want to?" He blinked back what I thought might be tears.

I paused, searching for the right answer. I wanted to and I didn't. I couldn't be sure. But I was sure that the way he was looking at me right then was a way he had not in so long that it caused the ache in my belly to rocket into my lungs and steal my breath. In that moment, all I wanted to do was make him happy.

"Yes."

After such an extended probation on intimacy, it wasn't surprising Joe's excitement didn't last long; if anything, that was a blessing. It wasn't awful in the way I had imagined the first time after the assault would be. He was gentle and kind. In any other situation, sonnets could have been written about his tender touch. Even the sounds, smells, and the motions of sex weren't exactly triggering. But what was, was the sickly sheen of shame coating my body when he'd finished. Shame at my own desire to enjoy it, to beg for my own release of pleasure.

Every day in the media, you can find depictions of young women who were raped or assaulted. Often, they are positioned in a shroud of modesty and virtue, as if the only way to prove their accusations is to prove their innocence. And yet, on the rare occasion that a fifteen-second clip from a story about a stripper or sex worker who had endured the same crime found its way on to the screen, there were always qualifications.

"She was asking for it, working in a place like that."

"What did she expect, dressing like a slut."

"She put herself in the line of fire."

Men could strut around golf courses and locker rooms bragging about their sexual conquests. They could write those conquests into the lyrics of their songs or their screenplays, essentially creating softcore porn for commercial consumption, and no one would bat an eye. In fact, the efforts were rewarded with admiration and praise.

But if a woman did the same? Slut. Hooker. Whore. Even in an era where the taboo of female masturbation had been eviscerated by the rise of sex toy consumerism, and Samantha Jones was proudly shown riding her sexual conquests into the sunset on nearly every episode of *Sex and the City*, everyday women were still lambasted for enjoying sex as much as the opposite gender.

And if you happened to be a woman who'd experienced sexual violence, you were held to a particularly wicked standard because society's continued preference was to see the world through the male gaze, one that still preferred innocence and obedience above all. And if you were a woman who chose to live outside those "norms," than you should be ready to answer some hard questions.

* * *

Afterward, I laid in bed beside Joe as he held me closer than he'd been able to in a long time. I could feel the weight of his body relaxing into mine, which was still rigid and curled in on itself. I wanted so badly to keep giving him that, to allow him to be close to the woman he loved, to give him the pleasure and attention he longed for. But I knew I couldn't, not yet, and especially not when the only reason for doing so would be to put his needs before mine.

I'd done it my whole life—let everyone I loved cut the line and find their happiness before I found mine. But I didn't have the strength to do that anymore. So I did the one thing I could think of in that moment: I told him I wanted to open our marriage again, that I wanted him to get back out there, find someone, and enjoy their company. I left out the fact that I wasn't near ready to cash in on my own hall pass.

I just wanted him to be happy, whatever it took. As I lay there awake in his arms, listening as he fell asleep behind me, I started to wonder if he would be happier if I wasn't there at all.

CHAPTER 10

Comatose

I'M NO BELIEVER IN GOD OR FATE OR SOME MYSTICAL CONSCIOUS-ness floating around and controlling the outcome of my life, but sometimes things happen that make you wonder if the universe has a sick sense of humour or just knows what's good for you.

John had been MIA since the night in the park when I'd blown off his advances. He hadn't shown up at Lakesides and wouldn't return any of my texts. The absence of his company wasn't as distressing as the abrupt cut-off of access to bad decisions. For the first week, I was desperate. Desperate enough to ask one of the bartenders if she had a hookup. Needless to say, I didn't return after that. Luckily, the worst of the withdrawal ebbed fairly quickly, just short of my attempt to hunt down drugs in my very white, very uptight suburban neighbourhood. Although, if HBO and Mary-Louise Parker have taught me anything, it's that I probably would have been successful.

Without the crutch of cocaine, I went back to consuming more whiskey and wine than a sailor on a cold winter morning in the middle of the Atlantic Ocean. And with that consumption came the return of the hangovers, a short temper, and a rawness I hated.

Joe had slowly started dating again. Even though I reassured him repeatedly that it was okay, he seemed hesitant to jump back in. It felt like he was always walking on eggshells around me. Normally, this would have made me feel guilty, but now it just irritated me. I was sick to death of being treated like some bird with a broken wing. Fragile. Something people had to handle with care. And what was the appropriate response to this irritation? Pick a fight, of course.

* * *

"You're not seriously going out again tonight, are you?"

Joe stood with his back to me as he spoke, concentrating more than normal as he dragged the razor over his jaw. I hated when he shaved his beard—his face instantly taking on a youth that, if I was being honest, made me jealous. It also reminded me of the boy he was when we'd met, still so full of resentment and anger. I preferred to see him as the man he was today. Matured, patient. Although that patience was fading more and more every day.

I ignored his question and changed the subject. "You know I hate when you do that. You look like a toddler." I pulled my hair up into a tight bun and dabbed a little concealer under my eyes. The allure of getting dolled up, even for a night out, had lost of all its appeal. The last thing I wanted to do was attract attention, but the dark bags that had taken up residence under my eyes were virtually impossible to ignore. And negative attention wasn't much better than its opposite.

"Good thing I'm not doing it for you." He shook the razor under the running water and splashed a handful over his cheeks before turning off the faucet. I watched him closely while he patted his cheeks dry with a hand towel.

An unfortunate consciousness was starting to surface again. Not the full-blown emotional mushroom cloud that had been hanging over my head since the assault, but splinters of feelings that popped up when I least expected them. Resentment. Jealousy. Longing. To my disappointment, no amount of intoxication slowed them down—and the frequency of their appearances was accelerating. The me before the me I was now would have seen that I needed to put a stop to the bad habits and face my issues head-on. But this me—the current me—knew I was walking a fine line between surviving and surrendering. And I was deathly afraid that one wrong misstep would send me toppling in the wrong direction.

"Who are you doing it for then?" I asked, folding my arms over my chest and leaning against the bathroom counter.

Joe stopped halfway through the door and turned to face me. "Me, and you know that. Don't try to make your shitty mood about something else. You were the one who told me to go out, to have some fun."

"You're right, I'm sorry. Old habit." I followed him down the hall, sneaking a peek into the boys' room before joining Joe in the bedroom. They were sound asleep, the soft yellow light from their bedside lamps illuminating the gentle rise and fall of their chests. I missed them. Even though I hadn't technically gone anywhere, I knew I wasn't as present in their lives as I had been. And that only made me feel worse about every decision I'd made since the night of the assault. Actually, if I was being honest, it made me feel worse about every decision I'd made *including* that night. Which, of course, only made me want to drink more.

Joe stood beside the bed buttoning his dress shirt, a rich indigo blue that made his eyes even brighter. "It's fine. So, back to my question, are you actually going out tonight?"

I wanted to say no, to beg him to change back into his sweats and sit in bed with me for the night, eating our weight in takeout food and watching bad crime procedurals. But instead, I lied.

"Yeah, John's going to pick me up once you get back from dinner." I fidgeted, arranging and rearranging the trinkets on top of our dresser. I didn't have to look up to know how my answer made Joe feel; the long, slow sigh was more than enough.

"I think you need to start seeing your therapist again."

My neck nearly snapped from my shoulders as I turned to look at him. "What the fuck does that mean?"

He rolled his eyes and bent down to slip on his shoes. "It means I've put up with this off-the-rails bullshit for too long. I get it, you're sad. You don't need to become a fucken alcoholic like your sister because of it."

My jaw clenched involuntarily and I had to struggle to release each word. "You. Do. Not. Get. It."

"That's not what I meant, Eden." Joe reached out and tried to touch my hand. I practically ran in the other direction.

I stood on the opposite side of the bed, my voice taking on a tone I didn't recognize. "You never say what you mean. It's always some bullshit response you think I want to hear instead of what you really feel. Which is exactly how we got here in the first place."

I saw his cheek flinch and knew I'd hit a nerve. I should have stopped, but I'd hadn't had a drink yet. Without the glaze of inebriation, all my pain was front and centre, searing the bottoms of my feet and filling my belly with a fire that scorched my insides. And I desperately wanted someone else to blame for it.

"If you had just kept your dick in your pants, I never would have agreed to open our fucking marriage, and I never would have gone out with that fucking monster, and he never would have done what he did."

My voice had pitched so high, so hysterical, that Joe rushed to close the bedroom door. We had promised each other that no matter what happened between us, we would never let our children witness it the way we both had with our own parents. Right then, though, I didn't care if they heard me, if the neighbours heard me, if the whole city heard me. The storm of emotions that had been restricted to the dark corners of my mind was no longer accepting confinement.

Joe took a deep breath and then slowly came around to the foot of the bed. "You don't actually believe that do you?"

In my head, I envisioned myself shaking my head no. I would run to him and sink into his arms, letting the dam break and all the tears, pain, and sadness finally spill out. He would hold me and rock me, and I would believe him when he whispered it would be all right. But that was a fabrication of my mind. There wasn't an ounce of me that believed anything would be all right, ever again. So instead, I raised my chin and looked him straight in the eye when I said, "Yes."

I should have done more to try to take it back. Words of apology babbled from my mouth, nothing coherent, but the damage was done.

Shoving his arms into his coat, Joe stomped down the hall and grabbed his keys from the hook before pausing in the front doorway.

"Please, stay home. Let's talk about this," I begged him.

"I've got that job out west next week. I'll be gone for five or six days. I think it's best if we have some space. We can talk after that." He turned and looked over his shoulder before asking, "Why can't you just move on?"

He should have expected the explosion of words that flew from my mouth as he slammed the door behind him. I, however, didn't expect his refusal to come home that night. Or the night after that. Left alone with my thoughts, that fine line I'd been walking between survival and surrender vanished.

* * *

The soft glow from the lamp on the little bookshelf beside the kids' beds cast long shadows across their faces while they slept. I tucked the blanket beneath Milo's chin and brushed the fine hair off his forehead. Leaning down and softly kissing the top of his head, I whispered, "You're one of the only things keeping me going, do you know that?"

I didn't wait for a response. He and his brothers were sound asleep, the rest of the house as quiet as a library after hours. Alone in the house like this, with Joe now gone for his job out west, my head was darker than ever. Like it was engulfed in a permanent cloud I couldn't seem to shake. Retreating to their doorway, I watched the boys and was overcome with a sudden wave of guilt. My actions hadn't only affected me; they had affected them and the stable life I'd worked so hard to give them. I felt selfish, reckless, and dirty.

After a moment, I closed the bedroom door and wandered down the hall to the kitchen where I topped off my wine glass, emptying the bottle. A splash of red spilled onto the white countertop and I just stared at it. I watched as it soaked deeper and deeper into the cheap melamine. *There would undoubtedly be a stain, even if I cleaned it up now.* I wavered between wiping it away with the palm of my hand and frantically scrubbing until there was no proof of my mistake. That's where I'd found myself lately—especially in the week that had passed since the fight with Joe—always caught somewhere between caring and not giving a fuck. Universal limbo.

Eventually caring won out and I shuffled to the cabinet beneath the sink. Reaching behind the bottles of glass and wood cleaner and boxes of garbage bags, I searched for the scouring sponges. Finally feeling them beneath my fingers, I pulled one from the pack and returned to the spot on the counter. As I started to scrub, the stain barely faded. I could feel the muscles in my chest beginning to constrict. No matter how hard I pushed into the counter, a faint shadow of the wine remained. I cursed under my breath.

"I'm doing everything right. Why can't I get it to go away?"

Deciding to try something stronger, I turned to look for the bottle of bleach. My arm collided with my forgotten wine glass and sent it careening to the floor, where it shattered into hundreds of pieces. I just watched as all the tiny pieces of glass skittered across the tile and eventually came to rest like freshly fallen snow on the dead ground. My lungs began to feel heavy, as if they were filled with sand.

I mumbled to myself again. "It doesn't matter anymore. Nothing I do is going to make anything better." I waved a hand over the splinters of glass. "In fact, it only makes things worse." Tiptoeing through the sharp fragments, I searched for another glass and more wine. To my dismay, the was no more. Disappointment quickly turned into irritation. I chucked the empty bottle into the sink, secretly hoping it would shatter as well.

Opening the pantry cupboard, I stretched up onto the balls of my feet and pulled out an old bottle of spiced rum with barely a few glasses left in it. I knew from experience that it tasted like cinnamon candy hearts, and I hated cinnamon candy hearts, but it would have to suffice. Leaving the broken wine glass on the floor and cradling the bottle of rum under my arm, I headed to the bathroom.

Once there, I started rummaging through a black toiletry bag on the shelves above the toilet where we kept any medications. It was never full, mainly housing expired bottles of antibiotics from past bouts of strep throat, half-empty bottles of headache medicine, and a handful of bandages, ointments, and hydrogen peroxide wipes. However, there were a few more recent additions.

Peering into an amber bottle that contained three white oval-shaped pills, I considered taking one of the anti-anxiety meds that my family doctor had prescribed when I'd started having trouble sleeping right after the assault. But they weren't fast-acting and likely wouldn't do more than make me sick to my stomach. Then I remembered something else I'd been prescribed. Holding up a clear bottle, I counted sixteen small blue sleeping bills—the ones the attending doctor at the hospital had prescribed for me if I encountered insomnia. The prescription had been for thirty pills, with one refill if needed. It had been needed, and now all that remained were these sixteen.

I thought about the relief that came when even one of these little guys lulled me into a dreamless, deep sleep, and I wondered how much better it would feel if I took them all. I had no memory of what it felt like to not be overwhelmed with negativity and fear and shame every minute of every day. When Milo's little hand held out yet another sticky Lego creation he wanted pried apart, no matter how many other chores I was already juggling, and I was forced to hold back tears while I pushed it away. When one of the boys would forget about my previous warnings not to sneak up on me and would jump around a corner, squealing with delight just seconds before I exploded into a fear-fuelled rant.

Knowing now how badly I was failing at the one thing I prided myself on—being a mother—was exhausting. It left me wondering what the point of continuing to trudge on was.

The idea of ending my life had occurred to me exactly twice in the thirty-some years I had been alive. That night, holding those pills, was one of them.

Palming the bottle and still cradling the last of the rum under my arm, I pulled off my heavy sweatpants and stepped into the empty bathtub in just my underwear and a baggy T-shirt emblazoned with one of the New York Public Library lions. It had been a gift from Joe when he returned from one of his away jobs, knowing how I had always dreamed of visiting New York someday and pretending to be the next Salinger or Didion.

Sinking to the bottom of the tub, I pulled the curtain across and nestled into the darkness. Following a big swig of the spicy liquor, I fumbled to pour five tiny blue pills into the palm of my hand. One would be enough to make me drowsy; two would help me drift off sooner rather than later; a third would knock me right out. I picked up three and popped them in my mouth, swallowing with another gulp of rum. Looking at the two remaining in my palm, I hesitated.

Sinking deeper into the tub, my mind suddenly shifted 180 degrees and I started to wonder how I could have missed the most obvious thing the night of the assault had destroyed. Myself. I had been obliterated. That fierce, resilient woman who had survived abandonment and emotional neglect and having to sacrifice her childhood to care for those who should have been caring for her? She was gone. And I was torn about whose fault it really was.

Chugging from the mouth of the bottle again, careful not to choke as the sweet, spicy liquid burned its way down my throat, I threw the other two pills into my mouth and swallowed. Leaning

my head back against the cold tile of the shower wall, I closed my
eyes and begged my mind to drift away.

* * *

*Laying in a very similar bathtub—on my back with my arms out-
stretched above my head and my legs under the tap as it drops chilly
drips of water on my toes while the shower rains down on my face—I
pretend to be a starfish. I am stuck to the side of a very large rock while a
storm ravages the ocean around me, and all I can do is sing a sea shanty
to keep calm until the storm passes.*

*Of course, I am just eight. I don't know any sea shanties except for
that one about Barrett's Privateers that every Maritimer knows, and it
isn't exactly doing the job of drowning out the storm—which is actually
the very loud, very venomous fight going on outside the bathroom door.
Kami, fifteen now, came home late again smelling of cigarettes and probably beer. And my mother lit into her, again, and the routine battle of
who could scream louder, hurl worse insults or slam doors harder begun.
Which was right around when I retreated to the bathtub.*

The tub had become a common hiding place for me in those
years, along with the back corner of our bedroom closet, the space
under my bed, and the woods behind our house. Like these other
places, the bathtub was always safe. I would turn the shower on full
force and pull the curtain tight so the only light coming through
was filtered through the orange pekoe fabric. Lying in the bottom
of the tub, eyes shut tight, I'd let the water beat against my face and
imagine I was anywhere else. Maybe an exotic rainforest. Torren-
tial spring rains would pummel the leaves above me before falling
down and cooling my skin. Or sometimes I would plug the drain
and let the tub slowly fill, paddling through the puddle as if I were
a stranded in the ocean.

There had been an escapism within those tiled walls that, somewhere along the way, I'd lost. Sometimes it felt like, as a woman, I'd
been born on the defensive. Back straight, legs crossed, head on a
swivel. I was so fucking tired of having to watch my own back. But
as I lay in that tub, letting the pills do their job and slowly giving

way to the foggy floating feeling, I found an unexpected solace in the thought that the fight might finally be over.

Struggling to open my eyes, my lids feeling as if they were made of cement, I fumbled around for the bottle of pills and, when I had it in my hand, gently shook it. All it would take was a few more and I could float away for good. But my blurry brain couldn't decide whether that was what I really wanted. It was a big decision, and I hadn't exactly been able to trust my own judgment lately.

With one hand gripping the side of the tub to steady myself, I struggled with the bottle lid, my thumb absolutely useless in the attempt. When I squeezed harder, the bottle just jumped from my hand and skittered to the bottom of the tub. I tried to track its location by sound alone, but became distracted by the repeated trilling of what sounded like a trumpet. Confused, I tried to remember when— if?—one of the boys had started playing in the school band. Or why they were practising in the middle of the night.

Tucking my feet under me and rocking onto my knees, I swatted the curtain to the side and leaned over the edge of the tub. A bright square of light blinked from inside my sweatpants and buzzed incessantly, seemingly the source of the offensive trumpet. A faint familiar memory pinged. *Phone. My phone.* I thought maybe I should answer it.

"Hello?"

"I'm sorry, babe. Were you sleeping?" Joe's voice was buttery with sleep, even though he was two hours behind in Edmonton.

"No, no, nope. Totally okay. Awake," I rambled into the phone, scrambling to grab at least two coherent thoughts to put together. "What's up?"

I heard him pause and take a deep breath. I was worried he could tell I had drunk too much, taken too many sleeping pills. I tried to remember how many pills I had actually taken. *Was it three? Did I take all five? The whole bottle?* I was so lost in my thoughts that I barely noticed that Joe had started talking.

"…know it's late but I just wanted to apologize for not saying I love you before leaving the other day. I'd say I didn't mean to but I did." He took another deep breath, this one shuddering a little bit.

"You don't love me?" My foggy brain couldn't comprehend what I thought I'd heard.

"No, that's not what I meant. I meant that I did it on purpose 'cause I was mad. I guess I was just trying to get a dig in. Which makes me sound like a child, and I guess that's right 'cause I just feel helpless. Like I want to help fix you but I don't know how."

His words started to punch holes in the fog clouding my mind, and I laid my cheek against the cold lip of the tub while I whispered into the phone. "I'm sorry I'm still broken. I don't want to be this way."

I could feel a wetness pooling beneath my skin, and I realized I was crying.

"Oh babe, I know, I know." Even across the line I could hear the remorse in his voice.

"I'm trying so hard to act like nothing happened, but every single day something triggers me or sets me off. It never stops. I'm letting you, and the kids, and everyone down. Fuck, I'm letting myself down." I couldn't control the sobs that bubbled up from my throat in between each word. "I don't know if I can do it anymore. I'm sorry."

"Please don't say that, Eden, please." His sorrow had quickly morphed into panic. "I don't know what I would do if I lost you."

The sadness in his voice broke what little of my heart that was left. In that moment, everything that had slowed started to contort and shift. I had been thinking so long and hard about what a mess I had made of the lives of the people I loved that I hadn't really considered if they would even miss me. I missed me.

"I'm scared I'm already lost," I mumbled into the phone.

"You can find your way back. I know you can. You're so much stronger than you know. How else would you have put up with my stupid self for almost ten years?" Joe chuckled through what sounded like his own tears, and I couldn't help but join in.

I wasn't sure if it was the sound of his voice or the weight of his words, but somehow my mind fought through the power of the sleeping pills. I clutched the phone tight as I pulled myself up to sit on the edge of the tub, dizzily swinging my feet over the side.

"I love you, Eden. You know that, right?"

"I do." I wiped the wetness from my cheeks with the back of my hand. "And I love you, so much."

"I feel horrible about our fight. I never know the right thing to say in the moment," Joe admitted.

"You're not the only one." I pressed my mouth closer to the speaker on the phone and whispered, "I don't blame you for what happened, Joe. No one but that guy is to blame." I took a deep breath and continued. "I'm just so mad, but I don't know what to do anymore, don't know how to climb back out of the hole I've fallen into."

For a moment, his end of the line was quiet. But when Joe finally spoke, he said exactly the right thing. "When I get home, we'll figure it out. We will figure it out together. Like we always do."

I had nothing to say in response and sputtered my goodbyes through a waterfall of tears. After he hung up, I took a moment to catch my breath and then attempted to stand. My knees felt like warm Jell-O. Stepping back into the tub, and with the curtain half drawn, I turned the shower on full blast and let the cold water soak through my clothes. The icy blast to my skin was like an electric jumpstart to my psyche, giving me just enough energy to shake the remaining fog from the pills and booze. I usually preferred to sober up with a greasy cheeseburger and an extra-large fountain drink, but this would have to do.

Carefully stepping out of the shower, I wrapped myself in a towel and shuffled down the hall to my bedroom. Standing in the middle of the room, with the overhead light brighter than I remembered, my mind attempted to catch up to my heart. Looking to my right, I spotted an old notebook on the bedside table in which I had started and stopped dozens of short stories over the years. Tearing a page from its spine, I rummaged through the drawer to find a pen. When I'd retrieved one, I quickly scribbled a letter to a later me.

You probably won't remember writing this but…

After I'd filled both sides of the sheet, I found a discarded envelope from an old stationary set and stuffed the letter inside, tucking it into a shoe box I kept stowed in a dark corner of the closet. Then I sat on the edge of the bed, the realization of how close I'd come to ruining everything I had worked so hard for slowly creeping in. Just an hour or so before, I hadn't been able to fathom continuing to burden my family with the heavy weight of my trauma. But now there was no world in which I could justify causing them trauma by selfishly escaping my own.

When the melodic trumpeting started once more, I jumped off the edge of the bed and hurried into the bathroom where my phone still sat on the edge of the tub. Assuming it was Joe calling again, I answered without the usual preamble: "Shouldn't you be sleeping, silly? I know I should."

But the voice on the other end was far more mature and carried a sharp edge. "Eden?"

I braced myself against the vanity. "Dad?"

"It's your sister."

It was nearly two in the morning in Halifax. The last time my father had called me with this kind of urgency in his voice, they had just dropped Kami off at rehab. *Was it another DUI? A relapse?*

"What happened?" I tried to keep my voice as steady as possible. We were the ones everyone relied on, the stable ones.

"She hasn't been feeling well for the last week, but things have gone downhill rapidly tonight."

"Is it her stomach again? She was taking a lot of stuff for her nausea." Since Kami had gotten clean, she'd repeatedly had issues with her digestion and even her organs. Now I was worried that the damage she'd done to her liver throughout her life was coming back to haunt her, and that it was finally giving out.

"We don't know." He paused a little longer than I was comfortable with. "We'll have to wait until she wakes up to find out what, or how much, she took."

I lowered myself onto the closed toilet seat lid. "Oh, okay. She's sleeping?" The silence on the other end sent a chill over my skin. "Dad? What are you not saying?"

"She's not sleeping, Eden. She's in a coma."

CHAPTER 11

Finding Purpose

SITTING IN THE WAITING ROOM OF FARRAH'S OFFICE BEFORE OUR appointment, I watched the late morning sun fall in streams between the blinds. I extended my hand out into the light and let the rays warm my skin. The first signs of a possibly early spring had started. Small patches of green pushing through the snow. The sound of birds chirping in the distance. More than a few hours of sun throughout the day.

I would assume that for the majority of people, it would have been an instant mood booster. And at one point it might have been for me too, but not this year, this spring. Not when I was recovering from a violent trauma and waiting to hear about my sister's health after she'd spent the previous week slipping in and out of a coma.

Pulling my cell phone from my purse, I swiped across the screen and typed out a quick text message to Kami.

2/26/18
OUTGOING: *How are you feeling today? Any updates from the doctors? If you're up for it, I think we need to talk later.*

Before sliding my phone away, I sent one last message:

OUTGOING: *Love you, sis.*

Dad had been sending me daily, almost hourly, updates since Kami had been admitted to the hospital—the same night I had to counter the handful of pills I'd taken with three cups of coffee and two Red Bulls just to keep my eyes open. Mom had been repeatedly asking why I wasn't coming home, no matter how many times I explained that I was waiting until it was absolutely necessary.

It wasn't like we were flush enough with extra cash to just jet off to the East Coast whenever we felt like it. Joe's business had taken off since we'd moved to Ontario, but with my retirement from the salon chair and only part-time hours at the yoga studio—not to mention our new monthly bill for my therapy—our budget was razor thin.

Which was exactly what I told my parents. What I didn't tell them was the real reason.

I was suspicious Kami had relapsed.

It wouldn't be the first time, and the last time had nearly destroyed our family and our relationship.

* * *

With seven years between us, being pregnant or having kids at the same time was an experience Kami and I never imagined we'd have. But the universe intervened and knocked us up at the same time with our youngest sons—Milo for me, and my nephew Roman for Kami.

Some of my favourite memories are from when my sister was pregnant. When she was expecting my niece Logan, she leaned hard into being sober. She ate clean and walked every day and waited excitedly to finally become a mother. It was very similar during her pregnancy with Roman. I wasn't sure if it was seeing her so happy, stable, and nurturing or because we were sharing this experience, but during that time we were closer than we'd ever been.

Which was why I agreed to watch Roman during the day a few months after he was born when Kami was finishing her college program, and why she offered to stay home for a modest rate watching Milo with Roman during the day and my older boys, plus Logan, in the afternoons until I got off work at the salon. It was the perfect arrangement. Who better to trust my children with than my family. Right?

I thought so too—until the day I came to pick up my sons and found my sister passed out on the couch, drunk in the middle of the day, while the kids roamed the house alone. That day broke us. I think it broke her too, because less than a month later she was checking in to a rehab facility in rural Nova Scotia. But in terms of our relationship, the damage had already been done. And it took a very long time to rebuild that connection. Which made it all the harder to believe this recent health hiccup had been an innocent incident.

* * *

"You mentioned over the phone that there was a family emergency that had kept you from your appointments. Did you want to talk about that?" Farrah asked, her hands cupped around her mug, the hot tea inside still steaming. There was no hint of accusation or disappointment in her voice, and yet I felt like a teenager who had been called to the principal's office for cutting class.

"My sister was sick." I said, absentmindedly picking at a hangnail.

Her stiff back relaxed an inch or two. "I'm sorry to hear that." She pulled my file from the stack on her desk and flipped it open. "You told me before that your family is back on the East Coast. It must be hard for you to not be there with them," Farrah said.

"I thought about going home. It's not a cheap ticket though. My father thought I should wait. Said he would get me on the next flight if things got worse." I inhaled sharply at the thought of what "getting worse" would have meant. "Luckily, they didn't."

"I'm glad to hear that." Farrah took a sip of her tea, relaxing fully into the back of her chair now. "I assume she's recovering now then?"

"She's been recovering for as long as I can remember," I muttered under my breath, peeling a small sliver of skin from my cuticle.

Farrah paused, then softened her voice. "You've also mentioned that your sister has battled substance abuse in the past, but to your knowledge was sober."

"And she swears she is, but I don't remember the last time I heard of someone taking too much Tylenol and it causing their liver to fail, sending them into a coma, just to wake up eight days later like nothing happened."

Farrah paused again. I had the feeling she was trying to find a sensitive way to navigate our first conservation in a while.

"What did her doctors say?"

"They did a bunch of blood tests and they all came back clean. They're chalking it up to previous damage done to her liver from drinking and too much Tylenol. Maybe some other underlying issues." I scoffed. "They're sending her home on Monday."

"You don't believe it was an accident, do you?" Farrah asked.

I snapped. Not at Farrah, but with the resentment I'd been pushing down and burying for so many years. "All I know is I'm fucking mad at her. Mad that she's putting us through this again. Fuck, I'm barely keeping my own head above water. I can't take care of her again."

"Is she asking you to?"

"No, but she has before. 'Eden, hide my pack of cigarettes in your Easy Bake Oven.' 'Eden, can I borrow a hundred bucks? I blew two month's rent at the bar this weekend.' 'Eden, if I pass out on this dirty couch in this stranger's house, make sure we get home safe.'" I ripped another piece of skin from my nail bed and watched as it started to bleed. "And it wasn't just her. 'Eden, make me a coffee. I'm too tired to get up.' 'Eden, go to the corner store and get me a pack of smokes, even though you're only nine.' 'Eden, keep it together, everyone depends on you.' I can't do it anymore."

"And you shouldn't have to," Farrah agreed.

I wiped the small spot of blood away with my thumb, watching as new redness quickly took its place. "But that's not how life works. There are the people who need and the people who are needed."

Farrah put down her mug and folded her hands on the table, leaning closer, making her presence more known. "Do you think there is nothing you are in need of?"

Before I could stop the words tumbling from my mouth, I laughed and said, "Sure, another drink."

The air in the room suddenly felt thick. I flinched instinctually, assuming when I looked up there would be judgment or disappointment written all over Farrah's face—probably the same way I'd looked at my sister in the past. That thought stung a little.

I scrambled to explain myself before she came to her own conclusions about what my comment meant. "If I'm being honest, drinking might be another reason I haven't been coming to my appointments. I fell into some bad habits. They helped numb everything, but they didn't fix anything and I didn't want to disappoint you or anyone else."

She sat back in her chair and folded her hands in her lap. "Who told you they were disappointed in you?"

I stopped fidgeting for a moment as I searched for an answer. When I didn't find one, I tried to clear my throat, which was suddenly very dry. "No one that I can think of right now, I guess."

She tilted her head and watched me for a moment. Probably surveying the contractions of my throat every time I attempted to swallow a thick, sticky gulp of air.

"Then why do you place so much blame on yourself?" she asked.

"I guess… it's just that this whole thing is really hard on my family, and I should be able to keep it together better, you know?" I shrugged and sat back in my chair.

To my surprise, it was Farrah's turn to laugh. She opened the drawer beside her and searched through a few folders. Pulling out a small white pamphlet, she slid it across the desk.

"Here, this is a support group for spouses of assault victims. Your husband can reach out to them if he needs to talk to someone. But you"—she pointed at me, looking down her sharply angled nose—"need to stop minimizing the very real, very traumatic experience that happened to you. Not your family. Not your children. You."

I clutched the pamphlet tightly in my fist.

"I know, and I'm trying. But I've found myself getting more and more angry lately."

Farrah asked, "Angry at whom?"

"At myself. That I couldn't protect myself better. That I wasn't in control. More often than not, it really feels like it was my fault. That if I'd been a better wife, if we'd never opened our marriage, if I hadn't gone on that date. If I hadn't been so desperate for attention…"

Farrah held up her hand to stop me. When I'd taken a breath, she started raising one finger at a time: "After a soccer game in the gym locker room, by a trusted coach. After having drugs slipped into her drink, at an office holiday party. By their own husband in their own home, while their children cried in the other room."

Her cheek twitched a little when she listed that last one, as if she were trying as hard as I was to maintain an even emotion.

"I've been doing this kind of work for two years now, and that is only a sliver of what I've heard." She reached across the table and grabbed my hand, squeezing it tightly. "Eden, it would not matter if you'd walked into that man's bedroom, gotten naked, crawled into his bed, and then said no. You said no. That means no. You are in no way at fault for what happened."

I hesitated a moment, trying to digest what she was saying along with the healthy helping of guilt it felt like I was constantly consuming. "But isn't it my fault for how I handled the aftermath?"

"No," Farrah said firmly. "The same way it is not the fault of a cancer patient when it takes months for their hair to grow back after chemo. You experienced something that changed a fundamental part of your existence, and because of that, you have been in survival mode ever since. The human mind will do whatever it takes to survive."

"I'm tired of just surviving," I whispered to myself. "Other than when I became a mother, it feels like I've spent my whole life just trying to get from one moment to the next. Just trying not to crumble under the pressure put on me to keep it together. Not having a purpose other than surviving is a hollow way to live."

"Even worse than surviving, you were just existing," Farrah reminded me.

I nodded my head. "Yeah, and I don't want to go back to that either, but I don't know what other options there are."

"Living," Farrah said, the word skipped from her lips, sounding like absolute music.

I thought about it; how magical and yet silly the thought seemed. *Weren't we all living?* I was breathing, getting older, but I had not been living my life in a very long time.

"What if I don't know how to do that anymore?" I asked.

"Then you'll just have to remember," Farrah said, pulling a sheet of paper from my file and reaching for her pen. "Like riding a bike. Try to remember the last time you really felt alive and start from there."

My mind filtered through memories.

Running through the wooded lot that bordered the property where I grew up in Nova Scotia, willing my legs to move as fast and as far as they could. Teetering on the edge of the old steel bridge in Shediac, New Brunswick, my cousin's hand in mine as we prepared to jump twenty feet down into the river. Most of the memories I could recall where I was really in the moment, living and not just letting life pass by, were from when I was a child.

However, there was one more recent memory that stuck out.

Lying on my side, my arms threaded through the rails of the hospital bed, I held on so tightly it felt as if the thick plastic might crack in half. Another wave of pain swelled in my abdomen, the muscles contracting and sending the pain out in new, searing waves to the rest of my body. Through gritted teeth I whimpered, counting the seconds. *One, two, three, four, five.* The sudden relief as the pain faded away wasn't enough; I knew another contraction was coming soon.

But when I heard a hushed conversation from somewhere behind me, my body filled with something other than pain—fear.

"The anesthesiologist isn't going to make it. He's been called into an emergency C-section."

"What does that mean?" Joe's voice quivered.

"She won't be able to get the epidural."

If I hadn't been hit with another contraction just then, I would have heard Joe curse under his breath, knowing this meant I would have to deliver our youngest son, Milo, without any pain medication. Nothing. All on my own.

When the nurses relayed the news to me and prodded me to flip over onto my back, I started to cry.

"I can't do this. I'm not strong enough."

One of the nurses took a look beneath my flimsy hospital gown and gestured to the other nurse to get the doctor. She placed a gloved hand on my stomach, rock hard with yet another contraction, and looked straight into my eyes. "You have to. The baby is coming and he needs you to be strong just a little longer. You got this far; you can do this for him."

The doctor arrived and sat between my knees, guiding Joe to hold one foot while the nurse held my other. She watched the monitor and started to count as the needle spiked and another contraction came crashing through my body.

PUSH. ONE TWO THREE. KEEP PUSHING. FOUR FIVE SIX. DON'T STOP. PUSH.

With every push, it felt as if my body was cracking in half. My bones splitting open and splintering inside me. Like an eggshell. Pain radiated now, with barely enough time between contractions to refill my lungs. It was the first time in my life I genuinely thought I might die. But even when my mind was ready to give up, to simply fade into darkness and accept that I would never hold my baby, that he would never know how much I'd loved him or how hard I'd worked to grow him inside me, my body refused to throw in the towel.

My muscles continued to contract tighter and tighter as my screams grew louder. Later, I would learn that Milo had been stuck, his shoulder turned and wedged beneath my pelvic bone. He was almost too big to be delivered naturally, weighing in at nearly eleven pounds.

What felt like hours later, I heard Joe's voice through a mouthful of sobs. "He's here."

Almost as if someone had flipped a switch, my body relaxed. My muscles melted into the stiff hospital bed and I released the breath I'd been holding. My mind had been positive that I wouldn't walk out of that delivery room, but my body did what it needed to do to keep me alive long enough to finally hold my son in my arms.

As I sat in there in Farrah's office, thinking—as she'd requested— about the last time I felt alive, I realized with a start that my mind and body had done the very same thing during the assault. Maybe I had managed to save myself after all.

* * *

Farrah's voice interrupted my thoughts. "Let's set our next goal—to get you experiencing life and not just floating through it." Turning to a new page in my folder, pen poised, she asked, "What are some things you enjoy doing?"

"Sleeping."

Farrah rolled her eyes. "Anything else?"

"Drinking and eating?" I shrugged.

"Okay, let's go back to a time when you afforded yourself a few more pleasures. When you were younger, what did you enjoy doing?"

I thought for a moment. "I played sports, went to the beach a lot with my family, spent an unhealthy amount of time reading."

Farrah smiled as she made notes. "I don't think there's such thing as an unhealthy amount of reading. What else?"

"I used to write a lot. Had stacks of journals and diaries."

Farrah smiled again. "The kind with the little lock and key?"

"Yes!" The rush of nostalgia made me a little dizzy.

"I had those too. My brother liked to steal them and break the locks off with a hammer." She held her belly, as if doing so would hold in her laughter.

"I used to hide mine under my mattress, but one time my mother found it." The shift in my mood sent me off balance. "She was really mad about what she read. It was probably one of the last times I wrote in it, now that I think about it."

"What we know our truth to be can sometimes be hard for other people to accept because to them it often looks very different. Everyone has their own perspective, but it doesn't make yours any less valid." Farrah took a small notepad from her desk drawer and scribbled an RX and two lines below.

I laughed. "What is this?"

"I want you to start writing again. Just journaling, twice a day. It doesn't have to be about anything in particular. Just pick up your pen and write down whatever you're feeling in that moment."

I took the mock prescription she had written up. "Do you want me to bring it to our next session so you can read it?"

Farrah shook her head and closed my file. "Nope, not if you don't want to talk about it. It's just for you. No one has to read it; no one will judge it. There is no right way or wrong way to heal, Eden. You just need to find your way."

It felt like a big ask, especially after I'd been lost for so long, but a new kernel of hope had appeared in the palm of my hand along with Farrah's prescription. I wasn't one hundred percent confident yet, but I held on to that kernel the same way I'd gripped the sides of the hospital bed as I pushed my son from my body. I was determined to do something other than survive.

* * *

After booking my next three appointments with Farrah—and prepaying as an extra incentive to keep me from bolting again—I made my way out to my car and dialled my sister's number. When she picked up on the second ring, I knew she'd been expecting my call.

"Hey, kiddo." Her voice was still raspy from where they'd inserted a breathing tube while she was unconscious. "They're taking me down for an ultrasound soon, so I've only got a few minutes."

"How are you feeling today?" I tossed my bag onto the passenger seat and flinched when it caused a travel mug to fall from the seat and clank to the floor. Sliding into the driver's seat, I still considered it an improvement from the all-out panic attack the noise would have caused a few months ago.

"Ready to go home. The food is terrible and I want a smoke."

I rolled my eyes, knowing she couldn't see it. "Probably not the two best priorities. How are the kids?"

"They're fine," she snapped, and I'd known I had hit a nerve.

An awkward silence filled the thousands of kilometres between us.

"What happened, Kam? What really happened?"

I heard her sigh. I guessed I wasn't the first person she had to defended herself to. "My stomach has been awful for months—you know that. So I've been taking Tylenol to try to cope with the pain and discomfort. Like I told Dad, I must have not realized how many doses I'd taken throughout the day until I started vomiting and feeling lightheaded."

I took a moment to digest the same story I'd heard from my dad, the one I hadn't believed then and wasn't sure I believed now. Then, I tried to choose my words wisely.

"Be honest with me, please. Were you drinking? Even if you had one drink with a few too many Tylenols, it could have made things escalate the way they did." I held my breath and waited.

"Are you fucking kidding me? Why does everyone keep asking that?"

"Maybe because it wouldn't be the first time you fell off the wagon and we were left to pick up the pieces," I shouted into the phone, instantly regretting it.

"Well, maybe if you and Dad and everyone else stopped putting so much pressure on me to get better on your timeline, I might actually be able to do it without slipping up," she shouted back. I heard a hiccup, her attempt to hold back a sob, and when she spoke again her voice quivered. "Even though that's not what happened."

I'd always been able to be empathic about Kami's struggles with depression and addiction, but I hadn't always related. In that moment, however, I got it. No one had been pressuring me to get better and put the rape behind me, but I had been pressuring myself. And with that, I knew I owed her, and maybe even myself, an apology.

"I'm sorry, Kam, seriously. That was a shitty thing for me to say and I should have believed you." I took a deep breath, steadying myself for the words I said next. "I do believe you."

I could hear her choking back tears. "Thank you." Then there were other voices in the background, probably the nurses ready to take her for testing.

"I'll check in on your later, okay?"

"Okay. I love you, kiddo."

"Love you too."

When I heard her end of the line close, I tapped the sleep button on the side of my phone and chucked it onto the seat beside my bag. I still wasn't sure what to believe, but it didn't really matter. What mattered was that she was trying to get better. I could hear it in her voice. And I figured if she could put in the effort, then I could too.

* * *

Farrah had suggested not just writing about the life I was living or wanted to live, but also doing things that reminded me of how it felt to live in my body before the assault. One thing I had always done with my body was move it. For ten years of my childhood, from five to fifteen, I played soccer. In my early twenties, after my first pregnancy, I'd started running—at first to lose the baby weight and eventually to quiet the chaos in my mind. And then I'd found yoga particularly restorative, which is a balance between the strengthening movements seen in traditional classes and deep, long stretches with a strong concentration on breath.

The practice room at the studio where I worked had become a sanctuary, but my fear of intimacy after the assault had tainted that sanctum. But when Farrah pushed me to retry some of the things that I had enjoyed in the before, the first thing that came to mind was my yoga practice. So the day after my session with Farrah, I took a chance and signed myself up for Janine's class.

Laying on my stomach with my arms spread above me, palms up, and my knees wide on either side of my hips, I inhaled long through my nose and held it in my chest while Janine walked softly throughout the class and spoke.

"Now, releasing this breath, let your pelvis sink even deeper into the floor, relaxing your hips and releasing all the tension you are carrying there."

Exhaling, I let my muscles melt into my mat, even though they were still a little stiff from lack of practice. Or the 400 tonnes of tension I was holding, if what Janine was saying was right.

Again, I track the soft padding of Janine's feet as she comes toward my mat. As a soft acoustic lullaby plays from the speakers at the front of the room, she bends and whispers in my ear, "May I?"

I knew she was asking to help me with an adjustment, meaning that she would physically have to touch me. Her quiet request for consent—such a small gesture, one she'd likely never even considered the power of—was all I needed to nod and relax into her touch.

I'm someone who would rather have her teeth drilled with a screwdriver than participate in PDA. Given that, many people find it hard to believe that touch is my love language. That, much like a puppy, I will gleefully accept almost any form of touch and intimacy from those I am close to. There's only one stipulation: It must be given without strings attached.

As a child, I would go for very long periods of time without physical affection, to the point that I developed severe insecurities around being touched or hugged or even holding hands in public. I think it was because these behaviours had always become some sort of show. To parade me around in front of an ex-girlfriend. To embarrass me with my discomfort in front of my sister's friends. To hype up someone's ego. Very rarely were there touches entirely for my benefit or pleasure. But as Janine gently massaged my neck and arms, I remembered one of the first reasons I'd been so attracted to the polyamorous life.

Joe had never been an overly physically affectionate person, and being a chronic people pleaser, I'd played along and pretended I wasn't either. But when we began to explore non-monogamy, I would experience these moments—not sexual ones but intimate ones that always left me craving more. Being wrapped in the arms of a partner while he ran his thumb over the soft part of my palm. Having my hair stroked as I laid my head in someone's lap and dozed on a slow Sunday morning. The weight of someone's hand on the small of my back as they guided me through a crowd.

There was so much I missed from my life before the assault, and during that class, I no longer felt selfish admitting that being touched was one of them.

After a moment of applying gentle pressure to my hips, Janine slowly removed her hands and made her way back to the front of the class before closing it out. Remaining in my prone pose, I slowly counted my breaths, concentrating on the memory of her touch, entirely unaware that rivers of tears had been falling down my cheeks. They made tiny pools below me on the mat, and when I felt the cool wetness, I swiped at my cheeks with the back of my hand. I had a quota for daily vulnerability, and being seen crying in public would have maxed it.

I waited until everyone had left before rising and prepping to leave. Janine remained behind, as she often did, to tidy the room for the next class. As I rolled my mat and wrapped the canvas strap around it, she approached me.

"Hey, do you have a minute to talk?"

I nodded, assuming it was something to do with the front end, and still a little flustered from the emotional release.

She held her palms together, her long fingers interlaced and searched my face with her cool grey eyes. "Are you okay?" When I hesitated, she smiled, warming the room a degree or two. "There was a big shift in your energy today. If you'd like to talk about it, I hope you know I'm happy to listen."

The impulse to decline her offer was immediate; I had to snap my teeth shut just to keep the words from tumbling out. It was a knee-jerk reflex. *Mustn't let anyone know you're not okay. Mustn't let them see your cracks. Mustn't burden them with your shit.* The classic responses that played on a loop in mind would have happily had me brush her off and change the subject. But there was something about Janine, the space, and the moment that begged me to unlock the barricades I'd put up and let someone, anyone, in. Plus, keeping everything to myself clearly wasn't working out the way I'd assumed it would.

So, I took another chance and a deep breath, planted my feet, squared my shoulders, and explained to Janine what I'd been going through over the past few months.

"Oh, Eden." When I finished, she held open her arms and, without hesitation, I fell into them. She rubbed soft circles over my back while I let the sobs that had been holed up in my chest escape.

We didn't say anything more to each other that day, just remained in an embrace until my body was completely exhausted and then silently went about closing down the studio. Before we left, she gave me a note with her personal cell number on it and a reminder that if or whenever I needed to talk more, she was there to listen.

Later, when I'd share the story of this moment, some people wondered why it was so brief. Why we didn't go deeper? The truth is I never thought about it. For me, at that time, it was more than enough. I didn't want to put on another show and dance about how traumatized or broken I was. All I needed, and wanted, was to be heard, seen, and embraced. Janine did just that, and it became a springboard into the next chapter of my recovery.

* * *

Later that week, I sat on the floor of our bedroom with various journals and diaries scattered all around me. By flipping through them, I was hoping to find some inspiration to start my new pre-scribed practice. But as I riffled through an old shoebox, something more recent caught my attention. A crumpled white envelope. Curious, I pulled out the folded piece of paper from inside and read the sloppy handwriting.

You probably won't remember writing this but…

The words on the page—seemingly written by a woman I didn't even know—broke my heart. I grabbed another piece of paper, a pen, and an envelope and set to work writing another letter.

You're going to need a reminder someday, and this is it.

Slipping it into the box next to the first letter, I make myself a mental promise to keep checking in on that woman.

Reaching back into the box, my hand wrapped around something much thicker than a journal. Retrieving it, I turned over the book to find an illustration of red cloaks and white hats staring back at me. Gold embossed title and the smell of worn paper. I flipped through the first few pages, *copyright 1985.* The year after I was born.

I could still remember the day my mother pulled *The Hand-maid's Tale* from the bookshelf that sat tucked against the end of her bed. By the time I was twelve, I had gone through every issue of *National Geographic, Reader's Digest, Baby-Sitters Club,* and *Nancy Drew* we had at home or could find at the library. And yet I was always hungry for more to read.

Even though there were times we didn't have enough money to buy milk or bread, and our relationship was more often rocky than not, my mother never denied my requests for books. Which was one of the reasons she had decided to hand me down the Atwood classic.

When my mother was up, it was like magic. We would sit in her big bed for hours, wrapped up in blankets and reading about magical realms, power-hungry villains, and futuristic heroines. She always encouraged me to read aloud, saying I had the voice of a storyteller. Our time reading together gave me confidence and comfort. Which made it all the harder when she was down, retreating under the covers, and I was alone again, missing her and our stories.

Maybe that was why I'd been so drawn to Margaret Atwood's books throughout my life. Not only did they give me a window into a world far worse than mine, but they also offered a subconscious connection to times in my life when things had been good.

I was still on the bedroom floor, rummaging through the stacks, when Joe came home from work.

"Where's everybody at?" he hollered down the hall. I could hear his work boots clunking onto the floor as he pulled them off.

"In here, babe. The kids are just out back playing," I called back, still a little in my head after finding the letter and the novel.

He sauntered into the bedroom and started to peel off his socks, dropping them into the laundry basket. "Isn't it a little early for spring cleaning?"

I looked around at the piles of chaos that had created a little moat around me and couldn't help but smile. "You know it's never too soon for any kind of cleaning." Plucking the faux prescription from my bag, which slouched on the floor nearby, I excitedly held it out for Joe to read. "My therapist has suggested I get back to doing more things that excite me and give me something to look forward to, rather than just scraping by day after day."

Joe unbuckled his belt and pulled it from his work pants, nodding, encouraging me to continue.

"She also wanted me to journal my feelings during the day, so I would have a place to unpack them in between our visits. That way I won't keep pushing them down. Which is why I got these out." I gestured to the journals.

When I'd finally stopped rambling, Joe smiled and said, "I missed you."

I tilted my head in confusion. He'd been home since the day after I'd found out about Kami's coma. He'd cut his work trip short and returned home as quickly as he could.

"What do you mean?"

"I missed this you. The happy, excited, full of life you." Sitting on the edge of the bed, he looked down at me with a soft smile. "I remember when you used to stay up crazy late sitting in front of that old white desktop computer we had, writing short stories. Even when you were pregnant or overworked or cradling a newborn. It seemed like a safe space for you to go and turn off Mom Mode for a while."

"I remember those times." I knelt in front of him and reached up to take his hand. "Even after pulling an all-nighter, it always made me happy."

Joe looked down at me, letting his eyes roam in a hungry way, and for the first time in months my body reacted in a way I didn't hate. "And you're so beautiful when you're happy."

Without another word, he leaned down and kissed me. His mouth was hard and wanting against mine, and all I could think about was how badly I needed to be close to him again. How much I missed feeling safe in his embrace. How I would give anything to fall in love all over again, for just a taste of that spark. Joe must have sensed the shift in my energy. We fell into bed and didn't surface until we'd both satisfied what we'd been longing for.

* * *

Lying in bed, I rested my head on his bare chest, the coarse hairs tickling my cheek. "I missed this." He nodded in agreement. Quieter, I whispered into his skin, "I missed me too."

Joe bent and placed a kiss on my still-tender lips. We smiled at each other, a moment of shared bliss that I'd almost forgotten could happen. It didn't last long. The sound of the front door being thrown open had us shooting upright in bed.

"Mom! Dad! We're back!" The kids called in unison as they came in from the backyard.

Joe leapt from the bed and slammed the bedroom door shut, yelling, "We'll be right out!"

I laughed at his attempt to shimmy into his underwear and pyjama pants as quickly as possible, hopping on one foot and then the other. It was one of those moments that felt so normal, so every day, and I wanted to soak up every minute of it. But I could hear cupboards in the kitchen being opened and closed, and knew there was a brood that needed feeding. Climbing out of bed, I searched for the clothes I'd discarded in the rush to get beneath the sheets.

"Have you seen my T-shirt?"

Joe pointed to the floor. "I think it's on top of all your diaries."

I playfully swatted at his butt. "They're not diaries. I'm not twelve!"

"Still, I'm happy to see you doing something you love again. Looking forward to something again." Opening the door wide, Joe threw out his arms as our youngest son came barrelling down the hall and into his embrace.

Looking forward to something. It was such an odd concept. I had been spending so much time looking over my shoulder, the past always nipping at my heels, that I had forgotten to look forward. Now I was finally looking up, seeing what was beyond me—a little like a horse with a carrot on a stick. I'd found a small reason to start moving forward, even if it was a gratuitous one. It was a little scary, but also a little exciting.

CHAPTER 12

Margaret and the Birds

IN THE THREE WEEKS SINCE FARRAH HAD GIVEN ME THE PRE-scription to journal my feelings, I had filled four notebooks, cover to cover. I never went back and read any of it, but it felt like some sort of cleansing ritual—like all the backed-up toxic shit I'd been supressing was coming loose and flowing out from my hand to the pen to the ink to the page.

It didn't take long, though, to sense that I had more to say than just what I was feeling. The cycle of just repeating the same self-blame, anger, and release over and over was cathartic, but there was more inside me begging to come out. Eventually, almost without realizing it, I had started jotting tiny 300-word stories in the margins of my entries. Those small stories turned into pages of longer versions: sometimes reimaginings of my life, sometimes romantic interludes, sometimes much darker themes, ones that I had to admit scared me a little.

But I also had to admit that being scared of something other than my own shadow was a welcome change. I imagined it was like the adrenaline rush people who jumped out of planes or off bridges received—that mix of fear and exhilaration. It was a little intoxicating. So when I'd filled those notebooks and felt stalled in my ability to create more dimensional fictional worlds to escape into, I started stepping outside of my comfort zone. Slow, tentative steps, but a forward motion none the less.

More often than not I found myself in libraries. They had always been a safe space when I was younger, and even now that I was an adult, they felt like a smart place to transition from isolation to interacting again.

The libraries in Toronto were vastly different than the ones I had grown up with back in Halifax. We'd had our small rural libraries that were nothing more than big, open office buildings filled with a handful of metal shelves and a few plastic chairs and tables for the kids. But the Halifax Public Library was something lost in time. Built in 1951, the monolith of stone and stained-glass windows had two floors—one up a grand set of stairs that opened into a circular room filled with windows and towering stacks of books. The other floor was the original basement that had been converted into the children's section with its low ceilings, oak shelves that filled the rooms with their rich aroma, and brightly coloured bean bag chairs, colouring tables, and wooden children's toys strewn in every corner.

To a child who read too many books by C.S. Lewis, it was the stuff of dreams. Many of Toronto's libraries were much more modern, all clean lines and an orderly aesthetic. This was especially true of the Toronto Reference Library. While it lacked the whimsical charm of the libraries of my maritime youth, it had an artistic vibe that I gravitated to with its red-and-white winding staircases, glass elevators, and copious study nooks that looked out on the five floors. It also boasted workshops with authors and editors that I would never have had the opportunity to participate in back home on the

East Coast. And when I found myself longing for a greater creative outlet than my journaling could provide, it provided the solution.

As a bonus, more frequent trips to the library had unexpectedly created opportunities to reconnect with the kids in a way I hadn't been able to since the assault. In the beginning, I'd barely been able to leave the house to walk them to school, let alone stay at the playground for noisy, boisterous play dates. When I'd been more concerned about finding the bottom of a bottle than finding the bottom of their toy bin, I'd completely shut them out. Closed doors, raised voices, and indifference bred by raging hangovers—even over what had been a relatively short period of time—had conditioned them to walk on eggshells around me. And when my sober mind saw that, it broke my heart. It also gave me a new perspective on my own childhood.

* * *

Sitting in one of the kidney-shaped writing nooks at the library, with my notebook open to a blank page before me and watching the boys skip from shelf to shelf, I had to admit that not everything in my early life had been as frayed at the edges as I remembered. Despite the late night battles, the often-empty cupboards, and the sticky nicotine stains on the walls, I could see that period of time through a different lens now.

My parents weren't perfect; they were human. And so was I—a very imperfect, struggling-to-get-it-right human. But my children loved me regardless, the same way I loved my parents despite all the ways they went wrong. This realization gave way to others.

If I had finally walked a few miles in my parents' shoes, and could therefore understand some of where they'd been coming from, then I had to ask myself a question: Why I was still afraid of sharing what had happened to me with them? It also made me question why, if my sons could continue to love me even after I'd been broken, taken from them, and brought back again, I couldn't find the empathy to love myself?

Declyn called out just then, interrupting my thoughts and pointing to a brightly coloured poster pinned to one of the large columns. "Mom! Look! It's for the Pride parade. Can we go again this year, please?"

I had been to a few Pride parades—those glitter-covered, loud and loving celebrations of the LGBTQIA+ community that took place every June. The previous year had been our first in Toronto, and to my surprise, my oldest son had asked if he could attend with me. He was only twelve at the time and, at first, I'd assumed he'd overheard me talking about the music, the dancing, and the drag queens and simply wanted to join in the party. But Declyn was the definition of an old soul, typically preferring to spend his time with the adults or shepherding the younger children around like a lanky nanny. And, true to character, his actual reasons for wanting to attend the parade were much more mature. He had started to question his sexuality. Feeling caught somewhere between straight and queer, he was curious about what that life was like. And since I still was not openly bisexual with anyone but my husband, I could understand why he felt the need to search outside of our home for answers.

I had never had that kind of opportunity to explore when I was younger and questioning, so part of my mind wanted to immediately agree. But another part was worried and overly protective. *What will he get out of it? Is it too much, too young?* Joe and I deliberated for weeks, weighing all the pros and cons. Both of us wanted to support his obvious interest in a world far separated from our suburban life, but we also wanted to keep him a kid for as long as possible.

In the end, we couldn't find a valid reason not to take him, and, on the day of the parade, seeing him openly embracing this new tradition made me swell with pride. I still felt like I'd fucked up tremendously as a mother since the assault, but maybe the damage wasn't as great as I'd thought.

That moment, though, was still a few weeks away. Back in the library, we gathered our belongings and I began herding the boys toward the elevator just as a somewhat familiar man approached quickly. Immediately, the hairs on my neck stood up, and I could feel the muscles in my back stiffen. This was the kind of trigger I had been terrified of experiencing out in the world, but thankfully, as he drew closer, I recognized him, and my warning alarms quieted.

"Brian, hello! Good to see you again," I greeted the slight man, his mousey brown hair a permanent frazzled mop on the top of his head. The first time I'd seen him, leading a creative writing workshop I'd attended at the library a few weeks prior, I remembered thinking he reminded me of a male Ms. Frizzle from the children's animated TV show *The Magic School Bus*. The workshop had been one of the first times I'd trusted myself to be in a room full of strangers for an extended period of time, and seeing a reminder of a favourite character from childhood made the experience slightly less scary.

"I'm happy to see you as well, Mrs. Boudreau." He nervously shuffled from foot to foot, his eyes darting to and from the pack of impatient children waiting to press the elevator button. "I see you've got your hands full at the moment, but I remembered you had asked about furthering your writing with more in-depth education during our class."

I nodded. "Yes, but unfortunately I only attended community college for cosmetology, and universities don't consider that adequate for an MFA."

He chuckled, his oval wire-rimmed glasses slipping to the tip of his nose. "Yes, they do tend to be picky about their applicants, but I did find something that I think you would be a perfect fit for." Handing me a printout that had been clearly folded and unfolded several times, he pointed to the faded font. "It's a writer's retreat, but not like most. You have to actually apply for it and only a select few writers are chosen to attend. The retreat is on a tiny island in the middle of Lake Erie called Pelee Island, and you spend all your time writing together in isolation and nature. But at the end you get to have your manuscripts workshopped by well-respected authors—"

Interrupting before he could continue to regale me with tales of an experience I'd never get the chance to partake in, I shook my head. "There's no way I'm the right candidate for something like this. Thank you, but I'm not a professional writer. Not even an amateur writer, really. It's more of a hobby, therapy."

He tilted his head and looked at me curiously. "The pieces you wrote in our class didn't feel like those of a hobbyist. They felt inspired by someone who had lived a life worth writing about."

Nervously laughing at his compliment, I shrugged. "It was just sloppy fiction, something that crawled out of my imagination and onto the page. A real writer probably knows a lot more about plot and structure. I'm not a real writer."

"Well, I think you are, and I bet she would think so too." He pointed to the printout again, this time toward the bottom where the text had been bolded: *Margaret Atwood.*

* * *

Serendipity is described as an unplanned but fortunate occurrence of events. Which is exactly what I was feeling as I sat in front of our outdated Dell laptop, sticky with yogurt fingerprints, holding the wrinkled printout Brian had given me in my hand. I continued to stare at the name of one of the authors who would be workshopping the attendee's manuscripts near the end of the retreat—Margaret Atwood. The other was also a very well-known and well-respected author, Wayne Grady, but for me, it felt like a sign that Margaret would be there. The only thing I had to figure out was how to get myself there.

The application required not only my career highlights (of which I had none), but also ten pages of a work in progress (of which I also had none). Although I figured it would be easier to come up with a solid ten pages before the deadline in a few weeks than it would be to make a writing career appear out of nowhere.

I pulled up the short story I had been working on during the library workshop, a dystopian tale of a survivor of sex trafficking who has to decide whether to save herself or return to where it all began to save others. It was clearly inspired by the fantasy and urban paranormal novels I had veraciously consumed during my younger years, not to mention my own current struggle with what life felt like in the aftermath of violence. The work thus far had also been motivated by the lingering notion in the back of my mind that I should be doing more than just worrying about my own recovery.

Finding a spot where it felt natural to start expanding, I set to work and, four hours later when Joe shuffled from our bedroom with sleep in his eyes, I looked up.

"You coming to bed tonight, babe?" We both glanced at the neon glow from the clock on the stove. 3:00 a.m.

I shook out the stiffness that had begun developing in my hands and saved the progress on my Word doc. "I suppose I should. Just got sucked into this story and didn't realize what time it was."

He leaned over and looked at the screen, his brows pinching together. "What are you working on? Something for the yoga studio?"

"No. Actually, it's for this writing retreat." I handed him the sheet. "The teacher for that workshop I took a couple weeks ago thinks it would be really good for my writing." Shrugging, making the sweater I was wearing bunch up around my ears, I continued. "And I think it might be good for my head too. Get out of my bubble for a little bit."

Joe scoffed. "For nine days apparently."

"Nine days?" I grabbed the paper from his hands and read it again. "That's almost two weeks." Crumpling the printout, I threw it on to the table and slammed my laptop shut. "There's no way I can be away from you guys for that long."

Joe reached over in the dim light and searched for the paper ball. When he found it, he went about smoothing it out. "Because you don't think you're ready to be gone that long from where you feel safe? Or because you don't think you should leave us on our own for that long?"

"Because I can't just abandon my family for nearly two weeks to go chase some stupid writing fantasy." I shuffled past him and headed for the bathroom. Standing in front of the mirror, the harsh yellow light casting shadows under my eyes I hadn't noticed before, I was caught off guard by how disappointed I felt.

Joe followed me. Leaning against the doorframe, he asked, "How long did you take care of the kids that winter when I had to work in Red Deer, during two of the worst winter storms we'd ever had on the East Coast?"

"Six weeks," I responded.

"Six weeks, with a baby and two toddlers. Stuck inside the house almost all the time because there was ninety centimetres of snow outside."

"Yes, but that was for work." I picked at a hangnail on my thumb. "Income we needed and…"

Joe interrupted, turning me to face him and wrapping his arms around my shoulders. "Right now, what we need is to find as many ways as possible to keep you happy. I haven't seen you this excited or, hell, even interested in anything in a long time."

I was afraid to look up and see frustration or pity on his face, or any evidence that he was faking enthusiasm just for my benefit. "But what about the cost? The time away?" When I finally dared to glance up, all I saw was contentment.

"You're worth it."

* * *

When I received my acceptance letter to the writers' retreat on Pelee Island a few weeks later, Joe was positive I was about to become the next J.K. Rowling—minus the rampant transphobia. Whereas I was convinced they'd had someone back out and just needed to fill a bed. It honestly didn't feel real, at least until the week before we were set to make the trip down to the island and the retreat director reached out to ask if I would be willing to carpool with another writer who needed a lift from Toronto.

The introvert in me wanted to decline. The recovering, easily triggered human equivalent of a trembling Chihuahua also wanted to say no. But the friendly Maritimer who really, really didn't want to screw up this opportunity before she'd even made it through the door of the retreat house eventually said yes.

"Thanks again for letting me tag along with you on the drive down." Mary, the writer in need of a ride, cradled her eight-month-old daughter, Aggie, in the crook of her hip while she placed a mug of hot coffee on the table in front of me. We'd agreed to meet for coffee before we hit the road the next week, likely so we could both assess if the other was giving off any serial killer vibes.

Admittedly, it was hard to focus on anything but Aggie's round cherub cheeks and dark doe eyes, but as Mary went into detail about her transportation predicament—they only had one car and her husband would need it to take their daughter to the sitter while she was gone—I found myself lost in wonder inside her Downtown Toronto space.

Floor-to-ceiling bookcases ran down one side of the small but cozy condo. A leather reading chair sat in the corner beside a window that spanned the whole back wall. There were picture frames scattered throughout, pages from magazines and newspapers ripped from the spines and hung inside.

Letting the warmth seep through the ceramic to my palm ground me back in the present, I took a sip before joining the conversation. "To be totally honest, I'm glad we're meeting before the trip. I was a little worried you might be a serial killer." I set the mug down with a satisfying thunk. "Or a mouth breather."

Mary leaned back and laughed, strands of her dark hair falling over her glasses.

"You're funny, thank God." Sitting on the sofa opposite me, she attempted to secure her wriggling daughter into a bouncy chair. "You never know who you're going to get stuck with at these things. One time, at a conference in Philadelphia, I was corralled into a group with this absolute raging misogynist who kept hitting on all the junior editors." She shook in mock disgust.

"Well, this is my first time at anything like this, let alone my first time away from home in years." I reached out and offered Aggie a finger. She pinched her brows together in a hilarious show of dismissal. I could see where she got her spunk from.

"Oh girl, I know. This will be the first time I've gone anywhere without my family since Aggie was born." She leaned in, raising her hand to cheek. "Don't tell her, but I'm pretty fucking excited to get out of the city." Mary glanced back at her daughter, and we both laughed when she received the same furrowed glare I had.

"I hope this doesn't come off wrong, but why do you even need this retreat? You've published a book, been in *The New Yorker*, *Maclean's*, even *Oprah Magazine*."

Mary eyes grew as wide as her smile. "It's fucking Margaret Atwood. Who wouldn't want the chance to have her give you feedback on your writing? Even if she tears it to shreds, it is worth it."

Margaret Atwood was this polarizing figure. She was loved or hated; there was no in between. However, there was very little disagreement when it came to the quality of her work. Even if you wanted to debate her stance on feminism, you couldn't debate how much she'd done to advance the reputation of women in literature. And, on a personal level, her books were one of the core reasons many women like myself and Mary, evidently, had started writing.

Unfortunately, that motivation didn't do much to dampen my feelings of being wildly out of my league in comparison to the other writers attending. There was a professor of English and German literature from California; a young, inspired contributor to a well-known, award-winning East Coast magazine; a bright young visionary from New York; a self-published grandmother from Alberta; and another Maritimer who was toiling away on her Masters of Fine Arts while simultaneously writing her first nonfiction project about the cod fisheries. Almost every single attendee had been published in some form, whether articles, thesis, or self- or traditionally published novels. And then there was me.

The closest I had to publication experience was an underwhelming mommy blog I'd started the year before we'd moved to Ontario. It was rarely updated, and when I did post something new, the substance was wafer thin. Hell, I didn't even know why I was really attending, other than to maybe absorb a few more skills by being in the presence of such talented writers. But after that? I had no idea what I wanted to do. For now, though, that was the best I could ask for from my still-wounded mind.

* * *

The retreat director, Donna, had strongly suggested we catch the 10 a.m. ferry from Leamington, in Southern Ontario, to Pelee Island. Apparently, the large vessel only made the voyage twice a day and the next sail wouldn't be until later that evening, meaning we would lose a whole day settling in at the house. Of course, to make the morning trip meant leaving Toronto at the crack of dawn. As a habitual road tripper, I was usually more than happy to get up and get on the road, but this was a little different than herding the children into the car with snacks and iPads and praying they'd sleep most of the way.

This particular road trip would mark the first time I'd been away from the safety of my home, my husband, and my family since the assault. So the good night's rest I should have had before hitting the road was more like odd intervals of fitful sleep interrupted by stretches of lying awake and staring into the nothingness, contemplating believable excuses to get me out of going.

Thankfully, the next morning before the sun had even crested the horizon when I'd picked up Mary outside her downtown condo, she accommodated my stoic silence with her own cheerful chatter.

She was funny and interesting in a way that wasn't patronizing but engaging. She did the majority of the talking during the trip, and I loved every minute of it. It kept my mind off the increasing distance between myself and my family, and when we finally reached the ferry, where I'd expected to tuck my tail and hide out in the car for the remainder of the trip, Mary took me under her wing to meet the rest of the group.

Sitting on two long green benches that faced each other in the centre of the upper deck, the group chatted and laughed as we looked out over Lake Erie. Anyone who paid even a little attention in fourth-grade Canadian geography knows about the Great Lakes. But until I was in the middle of one, watching the waves crash against the side of the boat and the blue horizon stretching for miles, I'd never fully comprehended their enormity. Felt a little like home.

Which triggered a homesickness I hadn't felt since we'd first moved from the East Coast. I wondered if it was for the water, my family, or just a sense of familiarity. I'd been unpacking more than my fair share of childhood trauma with Farrah, along with the healthy helping from the assault, but there was another side to those years. My house had been chaotic, to be sure, but it hadn't been a constant a war zone as it sometimes felt.

Almost everyone in my family was an artist. My father liked to pretend he was the exception, having become an engineer in his early years, but I distinctly remember staring in awe at the giant blueprints he would bring home from work and hang on his walls. They were as much art as any Picasso. My grandmother was known for her tole painting and cross-stitching. Kami took up photography, and both she and my mother actually attended the Nova Scotia College of Art and Design for a period.

Because of this constant mode of creation, many of my childhood days were filled with rock hunting on the beaches of Nova Scotia's south shore, bringing home buckets of gypsum, quartz, and fool's gold. In the summers, we would claim a spot on the side of Citadel Hill in Halifax and sway to the music of Maritime favourites like Great Big Sea or Ashley MacIsaac. There were road trips, antique shops, apple orchards, and hundred-year-old farms with Clydesdale horses bigger than pickup trucks.

But those adventures only happened in the upswings, the brief periods of time when my sister's rebellion was on hold and my mother's mood had lifted enough to allow her to leave her bed. Unfortunately, there were fewer and fewer of those periods as I got older. Which meant more and more isolation. Growing up relatively poor was bad enough. Who wanted the other kids to see your beat-up old plaid couch or empty cupboards? Add in a screaming match or anxious chain-smoking, and my home wasn't an acquaintance-friendly environment.

So, while the rocking motion of being on the water may have provided a brief hit of nostalgia, looking around at this group of women—women I'd been intimated by long before I'd even met them—brought me back to a time when being alone was my only option. It had been always been easier to stand on the sidelines and observe friendships being formed than to attempt to make them myself. Which was why I was so thankful for Mary. She was a pro at pulling me into the conversation, whether I liked it or not, forcing me to step outside my comfort zone. I didn't know it on that first voyage, but it was exactly the tough love I needed.

* * *

The first few days of the retreat were exactly what you'd expect: strong coffee, quiet periods of writing, and lots of wine. Since the night we'd found out about Kami's coma and I had lost count of my sleeping pills, I hadn't touched a drop of booze. Not because I thought I had an addiction—although I'm well aware that every addict believes they don't have an addiction—but because I was worried the smell, the taste, or just the sight of amber whiskey in my glass would trigger the memories I had been working so hard to flush out. I'd felt safe, though, with a glass or two of red wine as I read a good book or sat on the porch watching the sun go down over the water. Wine didn't hold the same power over me that liquor did, and certainly wasn't as enjoyable for shots.

The Bookhouse, our accommodations for the retreat, was a two-storey lake house with a steeply gabled roof, a wide covered front porch, and a cozy screened-in back patio that looked out over a sandy strip of beach. It had been redone on the inside to open the front room into the large galley kitchen and dining area, giving the entrance a wide and welcoming appeal.

The back of the house was separated into a communal living room and study area, with plush sofas and sturdy reading chairs. Books sat on every surface. It was located on a quiet dirt road on the east side of the island, with a small bakery and vineyard serving as the only real entertainment. It was quite possibly the most perfect spot in which to write. And for the first time, whether thanks to the distance from the real world or the seclusion from anyone I really knew, I felt like I was finally able to let down my barriers ever so slightly and see if the old me was still inside somewhere.

"So what's the plan after this?" Jenn asked as we sat on the foot of Mary's bed in our shared room.

It was nearing the end of our time at The Bookhouse and, to my own surprise, I'd grown even closer to Mary and to Jenn, my fellow Maritimer. Every time she spoke, it felt like home. She wasn't from Halifax—she'd come by way of Newfoundland—but that recognizable Maritime accent was regional and a clear signal from one East Coaster to another. From the moment we'd arrived on the island, I had gravitated to her—although it wasn't just her *by*'s and extended *o*'s that drew me in. She had a nurturing energy that radiated from morning coffee to evening drinks, and it was a welcome change to no longer be the only natural caregiver in the room.

Jenn tucked her feet up underneath her and poured herself another glass of wine from the bottle we were passing around.

"Well, getting a book deal for this novel with a huge publishing house and selling the movie rights—to become the next Atwood, of course," Mary only partially teased as she stretched out on her bed.

"I've got another year of this MFA, but I've been sending pages to my mentor while we've been here and they think it's close to ready for submission. So hopefully I can start querying it to publishers in the next few months," Jenn shared excitedly.

They both turned to me and waited for my response. I could have said, *I plan on going back home to arrange play dates and answer emails at the yoga studio*, but I didn't think that was exactly the answer they were looking for.

I thought for a minute before replying. "I've always thought that the time I took my oldest son to his first ever Pride parade, shortly after we moved to Ontario, would make an interesting story. Even at twelve, he was curious about his sexuality, and I remembered feeling that way at his age but not being able to really come out as bisexual until my twenties, so it felt like an important experience for him to have." I shrugged. "It's definitely not a novel, but maybe the start of a collection of essays or something."

Mary shot straight up in her bed and put her wine glass to the side. "Hand me your laptop. I know exactly where this should go." She smiled, the corners of her glasses creeping behind her thick bangs. "I'm going to give you a crash course in pitch writing."

Without so much as a question, I retrieved my computer from the bedside table and handed it over. Mary started it up and opened a new Word document. For the next hour, the three of us went back and forth on openings, the hook, a substantial midsection, and a catchy closer. After multiple edits and several more glasses of wine, we'd crafted three hundred words that somehow concisely summed up what I hoped the story would be—if I got the chance to write it, of course.

During the entire time I'd been on the island, this was by far the best skill-building exercise we'd done. But, to my surprise, Mary didn't stop there. She opened a new email window and typed in the address of an editor at *Today's Parent*, a very popular Canadian parenting magazine.

"Write out a short note just letting her know who you are, that you have a pitch you know her readers would love, and that I referred you." She handed me back my laptop. "Then copy and paste the pitch below your sign-off in the body of the email."

Laying my laptop on the bed in front of me, I stared at it. "Are you sure? I've never written more than a blog post. Do you really want to be vouching for me?"

"It's not like I haven't read your writing." She nodded at the stack of papers on the desks in our room. A critical part of our retreat was receiving feedback from the other writers, so we all had to read each other's submission stories. "Everyone has to start somewhere, and when I started out, there were people who gave me a helping hand. I'm just passing it on."

After thanking her repeatedly to the point of likely annoyance, I wrote out a brief email introduction, attached the pitch, and let my cursor hover over the send button. *What was the worst they could say? No?*

Since that was what I already expected, there was no reason not to. I clicked the trackpad on my laptop and watched as the email zoomed from my inbox. Then I drained the last of my wine and headed downstairs toward the sound of clinking glasses and laughter.

The next morning found us all nervously running from bathroom to bedroom, primping and un-primping, putting together our writing materials, and pouring big cups of coffee. Today was the day Wayne and Margaret would visit our little hideaway and sit with us to talk about our writing. Some of the women were calm and collected, but the majority of us were like fan girls getting ready to meet our favourite boyband for the first time.

You wanted to look put together and professional, but not like you were trying too hard. We were writers, after all. Or at least they were writers and I was playing pretend.

As I sat at the big kitchen table, listening to raised voices excitedly discussing which accolade they would share with our mentors first, it suddenly felt as if I'd been playing a part the whole time we'd be on the island—the stay-at-home mom turned wannabe writer—when in reality I was just a wounded woman unsure if she was still running from her nightmares or toward a dream. The other (real) writers had indulged this little fantasy of mine, but in mere moments, two very real, very seasoned and skilled authors would be sitting across the table from us, and there was no way they wouldn't take one look at my work and ask who let the fraud in.

That old familiar tightening feeling started in my chest and my breath came in short gulps, but before I could sneak away to find a bathtub to crawl into and hide, there was a commotion at the front door as a small blue sedan pulled into the drive. Everyone stood to greet Wayne and Margaret. I wobbled to my feet, willing them to stay under me long enough to shake her hand.

Margaret had brought her partner, Graeme, who was also a storied author with many bestsellers to his name. But when I saw the two sitting at the end of the long kitchen table, Margaret pouring a dollop of cream into his coffee with such care, I got the distinct feeling he was here for more than to just offer another critical voice on our manuscripts. Seeing that fragility and tenderness in a woman who was otherwise notable for her sharp tongue and very often controversial opinions made me take my seat again and plant my feet firmly on the ground. It made me wonder whether the prism of emotions inside us wasn't so much a flaw as a tool to be retired and returned to when needed.

* * *

During the two days we spent with Wayne and Margaret, each of us got the chance to go over our pages with them. Graeme wasn't feeling well so he didn't come the next day, and you could see a significant shift in Margaret's mood. She was a little more spunky and sharp. Wayne was a lovely contrast of calm and stoic, with the odd humorous barb thrown in.

After lunch on the second day, it was my turn. Margaret was reading fiction and Wayne was reading the non-fiction pages. So, I waited with my breath held while Margaret's pencil moved over the over the pages of my off-brand dystopian starter novel.

"You really like words, don't you?" Her fair eyebrow arched and the creases around her eyes deepened as Margaret peered at me over the papers. A few others snickered under their breath, but I wasn't sure if it was meant to be humorous or serious, so I answered for the latter.

"Well, I used to read a lot of Terry Pratchett, so that might have rubbed off on me a bit," I replied, and watched as Margaret's stoic expression morphed into a crooked smile.

"Well, you're going to learn how to start killing your darlings, but if you are going to choose the wordy route, at least really go for it." She flipped through the pages, landing on one and pointing to the third line down.

The line read, "She trudged through the waist-deep snow, cursing, unsure which direction was home but knowing she had to keep moving despite the frigid wind."

I looked from the page to Margaret and back again before speaking. "I'm going to be honest: I have no idea what you mean about either of those suggestions."

This time there were no snickers from the peanut gallery. Everyone intently waited for Margaret to speak.

She folded her hands on the table in front of her, the few silver rings on her thin fingers catching the afternoon sunlight. "'Kill your darlings' is a phrase coined by William Faulkner and is meant to advise writers to cut the fat, so to speak. To do away with unnecessary flowery prose that doesn't actually contribute substance to the story. Show us its bones." Again she ran a finger over the line on my page. "Cursed. You said your character cursed." Margaret looked at me, her gray-blue eyes intense and her head tilted at just slight enough of an angle to let me know she was really paying attention. "Why not just say it?"

I racked my brain for the answer I was sure I should have known, the answer every other skilled writer at that table surely was thinking—and now mocking me silently for being so ignorant about. "Say what?"

Margaret huffed an almost undetectable chuckle and said, "Fuck. Why not just say fuck? If you're going to be so precious about your words, at least go for it and use the really fun ones."

The room erupted into laughter, and Wayne, who had been quietly sitting opposite Margaret, shook his head with a wide grin. She was certainly the queen of shock and awe. Even when it was just a common curse word. Hearing it from the mouth of a literary legend and someone who very closely resembled my grandmother was enough to knock my guard down and let me truly step in to the moment.

For a few moments more, she called out my use of run-on sentences, poor punctuation, and lack of character development, but she closed her critique with advice that went far deeper than my writing.

"It's got flaws, needs a lot of work, but I'll tell you this…" Margaret paused as she handed me the pages with her faint pencil scribbles as a souvenir. "You've got the story. That's half the battle."

And then, just like that, she rose from her chair and wandered to the freshly brewed pot of coffee to refill her mug while Wayne started his round of feedback for the next writer.

You've got the story.

Rationally, I knew she was talking about the pages she'd just handed me—the novel I was writing about a woman running from her past, her trauma, not quite knowing what was coming next and forced to make a very difficult decision that could save her and others—but Margaret's words had landed like a thump on the back. Almost knocking the wind from my lungs and forcing me to take a step back to see things from a different perspective. I had been chasing purpose and direction, healing and hope, for so long that I'd ignored all the signs of a muse waiting in the wings. Of a story begging to be told. It was a story I hadn't known I had the capacity to tell, but Margaret did. She saw it in there, somewhere among the poorly written prose and pretentious language—a voice that could be powerful.

I didn't know where I would go from there, but what I did know was that I'd be a fool to ignore that voice now that it was found.

CHAPTER 13

Hard Truths

LESS THAN A WEEK LATER, I WAS STILL COASTING ON THE HIGH from the retreat, from Margaret's words, from being surrounded by so much creativity and passion. I was also a little jealous knowing that Mary and Jenn, and even Margaret, had gone back to their lives as full-time writers while I had returned to play dates, towering laundry piles, and answering emails at the yoga studio.

It wasn't that I didn't love the life Joe and I had worked so hard for. The privilege of being able to pick my kids up from school and be home for bath time and bedtime was not lost on me. But ever since I'd returned from Pelee Island, I just couldn't shake the feeling that my life was missing something. Maybe that feeling was bolstered by the fear that if I stopped moving, if I settled back into my old routine, the waves of trauma that had finally seemed to ebb just a little would come crashing back down on me and I'd be struggling just to survive again. But it felt like more than that. Like something was pacing in my periphery, just waiting to be embraced.

"So, Mary was like, give me your computer, I'm going to help you pitch this story to *Today's Parent*." Sitting on the kitchen counter, the cool surface chilly against the back of my thighs, I rambled on for what was probably the 700th time about the retreat. Joe stood in front of me, his arms crossed over his chest, and smiling from ear to ear. "That's like a legit publication. Not some blog I can throw anything up on. Seriously, just knowing they might even consider publishing it makes me horny."

Joe threw his head back and let out a deep, rumbling laugh—the kind I hadn't heard in so long it almost made me tear up.

"I'm so proud of you." When he regained his composure, he situated himself between my knees and ran his hands over my arms. "Making friends and taking big swings with your stories."

"The big swing was pitching the story before running it by Declyn." I rubbed the back of my hand with my thumb until the skin felt like it could ignite. "If he hadn't been okay with it, I would have killed it, but I highly doubt anything will come of it anyways."

Almost as if on cue, my cell phone buzzed in my pocket—just once, which meant it wasn't a call. Probably a text message, which I was happy to ignore with Joe so close and his touch soothing my anxious energy. But then it buzzed again. A notification I'd set exclusively for emails. It was my day off from the studio, and other than a school newsletter with bake sale updates, I wasn't expecting anything. Which was exactly what made me scramble to pull my phone out of my pocket as fast as I could.

Joe jokingly took a step back. "Wow, where's the fire?" I frantically tapped on the screen, opened my email, and saw a message—a reply bearing a familiar subject line. I held my breath and clicked it open.

Hi Eden, thank you for reaching out! This is such an interesting pitch and with Pride month coming up we would love to work with you on this essay. Below I've listed the proposed word count and rate of pay, if you could let me know your availability for a call...

Dropping my phone on to the counter, I covered my face with my hands in a fruitless attempt to hold back the hysterical sobs I knew were coming. Crying was rare for me, usually only brought on by intense emotion and, over the last few months, generally because I was on the brink of a full-blown meltdown. But this time it felt like my body was about to burst at the seams with excitement.

"What's wrong?" Joe grabbed my phone in one hand and gripped my shoulder in the other. "Eden, is it your sister? Is he messaging you again? What is it?"

With shaking hands, I turned his hand over and pointed to the phone screen. He was confused but started reading. When he'd finished, Joe looked up at me with his own eyes brimming with wetness and choked back a sob before pulling me into a bone-crushing hug.

* * *

"Yes, Dad, he's totally okay with being open about his curiosity around sexuality." I tapped the end of my pen on the hardwood reception desk. The class in session didn't end for another thirty minutes, so I'd figured since the essay for *Today's Parent* about taking my son to his first Pride parade was coming out in less than a week, I should probably share the good news with my parents. Only problem: My father wasn't much of a sharer.

"As long as he's not playing along just to make you happy. I can tell things have been tense up there for a while." I could hear the tension in his voice. When I had contemplated divorce years before, my dad had been the first person I asked for advice. But he would also be the last person to come right out and ask if my marriage was on the rocks again and if that explained my recent mood swings and distance.

Sitting up in my chair, suddenly a little uncomfortable, I contemplated how much I should share with him about the last few months and whether I was ready to share anything at all. I started with what seemed like the least terrifying confession—and something he would learn as soon as he read the essay anyway.

"He's not playing along; in fact, if anything it's brought us closer." I inhaled deeply and held the air in my chest while I blurted the next string of words. "Especially since I'm also bisexual."

There was silence on the other end of the phone, but after a devastatingly long few seconds, I heard him clear his throat. "As long as you're happy, it doesn't matter to me."

Like a cartoon character, I could feel my heart swell in my chest. I'd had no real idea what reaction to expect. My parents weren't terribly traditional or conservative, and certainly not homophobic or discriminatory, but my father and I had both grown up in eras when you simply didn't talk about these things. Private matters like sex, marriage, and money were meant to stay just that, private. So, the fact that he'd offered more than a congratulatory grunt and a change of subject was infinitely more than I could have hoped for.

"And being safe. Don't do anything stupid."

Just like that, the swelling in my chest deflated, and I knew that was as much as we would be sharing that day. And maybe at all. As I said my goodbyes and went about the rest of my day, I started thinking about the pros and cons of sharing. Even writing this one story about sexuality and freedom had given me incredible insight into the release that came with allowing myself to be so publicly vulnerable. But my words and their impact went beyond my own experience; they affected others too. They made some proud, some nervous, and some confused, and they would likely make others angry, upset, or maybe even offended. There was a fallout zone when it came to sharing, and I'd started to debate whether it was worth the risk.

* * *

Risk or not, the morning the essay was set to go up online found me perched on the edge of our couch positively vibrating with anticipation. It was a mix of pride at having shared such a personal and vulnerable experience for both myself and my son, and a healthy dose of trepidation over how it would be received.

In the months since the assault, working with Farrah had gone a long way toward helping me realize that my tough-cookie façade was actually a mask I'd been crafting since I was just a child. A way to protect myself from the pity or pain of others. If I acted like I didn't care, my young mind must have assumed that eventually I would stop caring. Of course, that was laughable. Even the most collected and self-assured people care how they are perceived. It's a part of human nature.

I impatiently refreshed the page every ten seconds until finally the headline popped up—"WHY I TOOK MY SON TO THE PRIDE PARADE"—with my name bolded below it on the byline. My squeals of excitement must have woken half the house and the kids came running to see what the commotion was all about.

"It's up!" I turned the screen so they could see. "My essay." Looking at Declyn standing behind his brothers, glowing with pride to see his picture below a paragraph, I corrected myself. "*Our* story." I handed him the iPad so he could read and then rushed into the kitchen where Joe was making celebratory coffees.

I wrapped my arms around him from behind and squealed into his back. When he turned and pulled me into a tight hug, I felt as if I just might melt.

"I know it's not *The New York Times* or *The Washington Post* or anything like that, but after dreaming about something like this for so long, and never thinking it would be possible because I didn't have the education or experience or skill"—I inhaled, filling my nose with Joe's scent in an effort to calm my excited vibrations—"it feels a little unreal."

"But it is real." He handed me a mug of steaming hot coffee and kissed me on the cheek. "And you deserve it because you worked really hard. I haven't seen you spend that many late nights or early mornings at the computer in a long time. It's obviously something you really wanted."

Taking a sip, I let the bitter brew rest on my tongue for just a moment. It seemed like so many important and pivotal memories were paired with the sweet bitterness of coffee. The way I loved it even if it burned. How if it grew cold and was left unattended, I never threw it away but instead gave it another chance to warm me. It felt like kismet.

"I did really want it. In fact, I still do." I was hesitant. Since well before I'd even returned from the retreat, I had been thinking of how to approach something with Joe, but had never found what seemed like the right time. Now seemed like it could be right. "What do you think about me pursuing writing? Like, making an actual career out of it."

Joe's face immediately sank. "You want to quit working at the studio?"

"No, no. That's not what I mean."

"Oh, thank goodness." He mockingly placed his hand over his heart as if he were experiencing palpitations. "Thought this was another all-or-nothing fixation again."

I laughed, pretending to be shocked and insulted. Truth was he knew me better than almost anyone and was aware that I had a tendency to hyperfocus on new interests, skills, and hobbies for about 10.6 milliseconds before abandoning them and wondering why I'd even been interested in the first place. This was even more the case when I was struggling with something. It was like my brain's primitive way of distracting me. Problem was it also often distracted me from other things—like working to pay the bills.

"Are you trying to insinuate I don't stick with things? Hate to remind you, I was behind the chair for nearly a decade." Propping my hand on my hip, I attempted to look seductively pouty, but may have landed instead on juvenile.

Joe leaned back against the counter and started counting on his fingers. "Oil painting. Macrame. Nutritionist training. Furniture restoration. Extreme trail running."

"Hey." I poked him in the belly. "That last one I'm still working on. I just have to get the guts up to get back out running."

He chuckled and squeezed my hand. "You have to admit, when you're avoiding dealing with things, you tend to bury yourself in hobbies."

I tried to ignore the pang of resentment that his comment stirred up. "It wouldn't be a hobby. This is something I've wanted to do since I was a kid. You know that."

"I do, but I thought you liked writing that romance fiction or fantasy stuff."

"And I did. Still do, I mean." I could feel my temper rising a little. *Why can't he just accept that this is something that would make me happy? Isn't that what he and Farrah and everyone are pushing me to be—happy?* "Maybe I'll write that stuff again someday, but this, this feels important. Like it's more than just a story. Like it means something."

I could feel a lump forming in the back of my throat when Declyn joined us in the kitchen, handing me the iPad because a notification had come in. Excusing myself from our conversation—which judging by the look of relief on Joe's face, he was perfectly fine with—I swiped over the screen to bring up the notification again. It was a new message on a long-ignored professional social media platform. At first I just assumed it was spam, but curiosity got the best of me and I decided to check anyways.

Hello—may I ask if you were the pen of the article in Today's Parent, "Why I took my son to the Pride parade"?

Hoping so, I just want to say thank you. At a time of crazy divisiveness within the US, not to mention our Administration even muttering insane comments about our northern family, I just want to applaud you, your family, and your message that you send to parents and children of all. I don't have kids, and won't, but think about how parenting like yours and your husbands' will make people like me feel normal. I looked for two decades for acceptance from my family, which you seem to have given your son without thinking and instantaneously. Truly just a heartfelt thank you from a Coloradan, for raising children now to see no difference, and understand, all are human. Thank you for supporting your son—who if studies are correct, will most likely identify straight. HOWEVER—the fact he knows it's ok to be—whatever he is—the World would be better off if all parents would parent like you. I don't write many, if ever, but was moved by the story, and couldn't help but send a pat on the back. WAY TO GO. Thank you.

It was only when I'd finished reading the email that I became aware of the streams of tears running down my cheeks. The other kids shuffled into the kitchen, impatiently waiting for the chocolate chip pancakes I'd promised them earlier. But Milo stopped and tilted his little head, examining my face. He gestured for me to bend down and, when I did, traced his finger down my cheek, scooping up one of my tears, and said, "Mommy, I thought you were all done crying."

It hit me right in the gut that my struggle had not gone unnoticed. It broke my heart to think that he had been worried for me, even for a moment. I brushed the wetness from my face and gave his messy bedhead a fluff. "Don't worry, Bean, these are happy tears." He tilted his head, smiled, and replied, "Okay." Then bounded off to pursue his breakfast. Again, there was that fallout.

I knew the story would affect my family, who would read it and have to rationalize what they knew and what they didn't. I was also aware people I didn't even know would read it, and maybe even a few parents would relate it to their own choices with their children. But never in my wildest dreams had I considered how it might change the dynamic of my own home or resonate with someone personally in the LGBTQIA+ community who had not been supported this way by their own family. I had been so worried about the carnage that might come from telling our story, but instead, it had reached someone I hadn't even known needed it. I thought, *Maybe that's what my story is meant to do.*

* * *

"So how did it make you feel to be so open with strangers about something so personal?" Farrah asked as she sat across from me, cradling her mug of tea.

"At first it scared the shit out of me. Everyone has an opinion and seems to feel the need to share it whether you want it or not, and so often it's cruel." I rolled the last few drops of water around the bottom of my paper cup. Sometimes I envied Farrah's stillness, and sometimes I promised myself I would achieve the same someday.

"Which is probably why you still haven't told the rest of your family or friends about the assault, right?" Farrah had a way of just cutting through the bullshit that I admired.

"That's definitely a big part. It's scary to think they might be disappointed or ashamed of my lifestyle." I made little bunny ears with my fingers to insinuate quotations around the last word. Polyamory had never felt like the alternative lifestyle the media or society made it out to be. It always felt like a natural progression for us—two people whose needs and wants ebbed and flowed during the span of time we'd been together. Not everyone wants to eat mac and cheese for dinner every night for half their lives. But when they go out to a restaurant or try a new recipe, they aren't slut-shamed for it. Funny how that works.

"Are your parents fairly conservative when it comes to sex and sexuality?" Farrah asked.

"That's the thing, I don't think they are. My dad had a stack of *Hustler* magazines with variations of a half-naked Pamela Anderson on them that he just left in a box where we easily, and often, found them." I chuckled at the memory. "And my mother, when she was present, was always encouraging us to inquire and educate ourselves on sexuality."

Farrah leaned forward and set her mug aside. "So what is it you are afraid they would be ashamed of?"

After a moment of contemplation, I answered: "That I was stupid and selfish and put myself in harm's way."

I could see the muscles around Farrah's mouth tighten, creating fine lines in her pale pink lips. "Do you truly believe they would feel that way? Or is there a part of you that still feels responsible for what happened?"

Shaking my head, I didn't have to think long about the question. "No, I don't think they would, and I don't know if I even do. All I know is I'm still mad. At the person who did this to me, and maybe a little at myself for playing whatever part in it that I did. I'm mad I lost so much time with the kids, with my husband." I chuffed a quiet laugh. "Mad that I can't fuck the way I used to."

Farrah had taken a sip of her tea in that moment and nearly spit it back out onto both of us. Stifling her laughter, she reached for a tissue to dab at her chin where some of the tea had escaped. When she was able to speak again, her candor surprised me. "Sexual health is a big part of the recovery process, and one I personally don't think we focus enough on." She glanced at the clock on her wall before adding, "If that is something you would like to talk more about at our next session, I would be more than happy to."

"I would like that."

I stood and gathered my bag, ready to head for the door. But before I could go, Farrah touched my shoulder lightly and asked, "Have you ever considered writing about your recovery, or even the struggle to rediscover your sex life?"

I paused for a moment, feeling a little vulnerable at the thought. "I guess I've toyed with the idea, but I've never really zeroed in on those kinds of specifics. It's a little scary."

She nodded and gave my shoulder a squeeze. "That's completely valid. The only reason I ask is because of the purpose and joy you seem to have gained from writing your first essay. It seems to be very cathartic, and I personally know several survivors who have done similar things, usually anonymously, and found it hugely helpful in their healing."

"Anonymously." I rolled the word around my mouth and decided to chew on it a little.

"Just something to think about—and certainly not until you're ready."

That night when I returned home, and to my own surprise, I almost immediately planted myself in front of the computer. I wasn't sure where to start with the pitch, or even the story, but Farrah's words echoed in my mind: *Not until you're ready.* It felt a little like I was flying blind, but I was surer than ever that I was ready to do so.

An hour or so later, I had it. Three hundred polished words that would hopefully grab the attention of the editor at the women's magazine, *Flare*, whose email I was pasting into the recipient box. The magazine had published three other stories by anonymous women who had been victims of rape or sexual violence, so it felt like a perfect fit. But even as my cursor hovered over the signature line, I knew that they might see my non-monogamous marriage as complicating the "innocent victim" narrative, and I contemplated sending it anonymously as well.

But sitting alone in the dark of my kitchen, all I could think about was how much I wanted someone to share this moment with. Someone who understood the complexities of trauma and recovery, and was not just offering empathy. If I sent my pitch anonymously, and they did choose to pick it up, my story would be just one more faceless addition to a never-ending parade of stories. I wanted to do more than lend my voice.

Typing my name at the bottom of the email, I tapped the trackpad and watched as the message zoomed from my inbox and hopefully into acceptance.

* * *

Even though I was still incredibly hesitant about meeting someone new, when I decided to take the plunge and redownload a popular dating app, I chose to start with potential partners I knew I would be the most comfortable with—women. I had no expectations, but the moment I came across the profile of Anna—a dark-haired beauty who was proudly Italian and proudly gay with doe-like chestnut eyes and a smile that felt like a gut punch when I looked at it, in the best way—I felt a spark of excitement. I can still distinctly remember sitting on our back porch, the evening growing dark and the early summer air still warm enough to shed my sweater. Holding my breath as my finger hovered over the like icon, a bright red heart. Tapping the screen and feeling my pulse hiccup when a blinking star indicated that we had matched.

There was a mix of fear and anticipation as I watched the little blue dots bounce at the bottom of the text box, waiting for her first message. It was reminiscent of the notes passed on playgrounds and tender words whispered in ears in the dark corners of smoky bars. That was when I realized exactly how much I had missed the exhilaration of connecting with someone new. Yet another thing I could curse my attacker for taking from me, even if only for a few months.

For the rest of the night and nearly every minute of the next week, Anna and I spoke non-stop about life, loves, friends, and vices. The night before we had agreed to go on our first date, I dared myself to be excited. Unfortunately, the next morning, even the excitement couldn't tune out the fear.

Statistically, I was nowhere near as likely to be assaulted by a woman as I was by a man. Especially one who was nearly three inches shorter and a hundred pounds lighter. But as Farrah constantly reminded me, our primitive brain, the one that stores traumatic memories in order to keep us safe, sometimes doesn't subscribe to statistics or even rationality. Which fostered my decision to take the train to meet in Downtown Toronto, not far from her neighbourhood but in a busy spot just off Bloor Street with plenty of bustling lunch spots to choose from. It felt safe and smart, but I couldn't help reminding myself that I had also felt this way the night I met Liam.

But after a long, conversation-heavy lunch and a wander through the downtown streets, it was clear this experience was far from my last.

"I'm really glad you came all this way to meet me." Anna reached across the small distance between us and interlaced her fingers with mine. My skin reacted in a wave of goosebumps and I tried to contain the shivers she gave me. "But I've got to be honest, I've never dabbled in the poly life."

"Oh no?" I tightened my grip on her hand, already knowing where the conversation was heading but hoping to savour the moment as long as I could.

"Nah, I think I'm a pretty clichéd lesbian." When I pinched my face up in question, she continued, "You know, like the joke: What does a lesbian bring to a second date?" I shook my head, unsure of the punchline. She threw her head back and laughed at my innocence. "A U-Haul! We tend to fall into monogamy and commitment pretty quick."

I laughed along with her, and even though I was a little deflated, I wasn't shocked or even terribly disappointed. Meeting Anna was beautiful, and it was also a step back into the life I once had. The life I had been craving a return to more and more.

Another step forward, or back into the life I'd been living before the assault—however you want to see it—was the phone call I received a few weeks after my slow introduction back into dating.

* * *

"Hi, is this Eden?" a sing-songey voice asked on the other end of the line.

"It is."

I tried to temper the excitement in my voice. The day before—and a few weeks after I'd submitted my pitch—I had received an email from the editor at *Flare* magazine, Ishani Nath, asking if I was available for a phone call. It wasn't the immediate acceptance I'd received for my first essay, and part of me worried I'd made some sort of pitching faux pas and she wanted to chew me out for my ignorant mistake.

"Thank you for making the time to hop on the phone with me today. First thing I want to say is"—I held my breath waiting for the axe I was sure would drop on my head any moment—"I hope you know how incredibly brave you are for wanting to tell your story. It cannot have been an easy decision."

Truth was I still wasn't entirely sure it was the right decision. It hadn't so much been a decision as a gut feeling that I needed to follow in order to continue moving forward.

"Thank you, I'm still considering pretending it was all a poorly orchestrated joke, but I figure it's better to see it through," I teased, forcing a nervous laugh so she understood I wasn't just wasting her time.

"Well, I'm glad to hear that, because the second reason I'm calling today is to tell you that we are very, very interested in running your story."

For a millisecond after Ishani spoke, I had to grip the porch railing to keep the ground from falling out from beneath me.

"You want to publish my essay? Really?" I tried my hardest not to stutter, even though the lump in the back of my throat was alerting me that tears could be on the way.

"Of course! It's a very important story, and you have a truly unique perspective, being that you were in a non-monogamous marriage when the assault occurred." Her excited tone took on a hint of seriousness. "The only real question is, do you want to write it anonymously or under your name?"

Again, I was forced to pause. I had gone back and forth so many times about whether I would use my name if I ever went public with my story after Farrah and I had talked about it. The truth was I was still afraid. Afraid he might see it and find me. Afraid parents from the kids' school would read it and treat them differently because they thought their mom was a "whore." Afraid that people would think I was lying.

Ishani interrupted my thoughts. "If you do choose to use your name, I can guarantee you will be helping many women be a little braver to tell their story as well."

That was it. It was all I needed to surpass the crippling fear. It wasn't the first time I had been told that speaking out would help others, but it would be the first time I had the guts to go through with it.

"Yes," I inhaled deeply. "I want to use my name, especially if it could help anyone."

Ishani enthusiastically thanked me and we made plans to talk later in the week about the editor I would be working with, a word count, a delivery date I'd be comfortable with, and what photos we could use. After hanging up, I sat on the cool stone steps for several moments, letting the morning sun warm my knees. There was a part of me that was vibrating with excitement, that wanted to run inside and scream the news to Joe. That was luxuriating in the reality that my first essay hadn't just been a fluke and that maybe, just maybe, I could make this professional writing thing work.

But there was another, much louder part that knew I hadn't just agreed to share my story with Ishani's readers. Whether I was ready or not, I would be sharing it with really anyone who knew me and had access to the internet. And it wasn't exactly something I imagined any parent wanting to find out about from a women's magazine. I slipped off my sandals and planted my feet firmly on the step below me, raised my chest, pulled back my shoulders, and tapped the screen on my phone, holding my breath as it rang.

* * *

"So, you're not getting a divorce." My father paused, and I could envision his thick charcoal-grey brows pinching together as he tried to rationalize what I had just told him. "But you are seeing other people?"

I chuckled, more a nervous response than out of humour. "No, I mean, yeah. Kind of. But not like we're separated. We're actually really happy. Way more so than in the early years. We just decided to have a non-monogamous marriage, and it's been working for us for a few years now."

The silence on the other end of the line made my stomach drop.

My father and I had always been close. Sometimes I thought we were too alike not to be. But when I was a child, he'd spent so much time attempting to keep Kami on the straight and narrow—to make up for, in his mind, the disservice of leaving his marriage with my mother and ultimately leaving my sister—that I often felt as if I was fighting for his attention. That I was jumping up and down, my little blond pigtails and chubby cheeks bouncing as I waved my hands over my head, yelling, "Pick me! Pick me!"

Since moving to Ontario there had been a shift. I wasn't sure if the distance finally gave him the motivation to reach out or if he'd been trying to catch up with me for years and I'd finally noticed, but we were closer than ever before. As I waited for his response to only the first of the two very difficult conversations we needed to have, I truly feared I would lose everything we'd gained.

When he finally replied, his tone was curt. "Do the kids know?"

"No, of course not. They're too young for that conversation." Which, if I was being honest, felt a little hypocritical considering the openness we had about sexuality, but that was an argument for another time.

"Is he respecting the rules and restrictions you have set for him?" There was a sharpness in his voice that he often hid. I knew he cared for Joe. He'd never had a son himself, and I'm sure that when Joe and I married he'd considered it a happy addition. But anyone who hurt his daughters immediately lost all his respect, and I think he was contemplating the impact of this news on Joe's score with him.

"Yes. He's actually been much more open, and he communicates when he's feeling off instead of just heading to the strip club." I tried to lighten the mood but wasn't sure how it would land. To my surprise, when my father spoke again his tone was just a hair lighter.

"As long as you're happy, and the kids are happy." He paused, and I could hear him sigh. "Frankly, you're already doing better than half the people your age, divorced and on to their second failed marriages. If it works for you and doesn't hurt anyone then you must be doing something right. And the reality is, how you live your life is no one's business anyway."

Here was where I had to sigh. "That is, of course, unless I make it everyone's business by writing about it publicly."

"Yes, well there is that. Has he told his family?"

I picked at a flaking piece of paint on the railing, "He plans to, shortly before the article comes out. It's mostly about my journey back to a healthy, umm, intimate relationships after..." As my words trailed off, I realized this was it, that it was now or never. "After being sexually assaulted."

CHAPTER 14

Don't Read the Comments

Have you filed a report?

It was the first question out of both my father's and, later, my mother's mouth when I told them about the assault. When I told them I hadn't, their second question was *Why?* I could have given them a thousand reasons—probably could have made a PowerPoint presentation on why reporting sexual violence felt useless—but I knew what they were really asking was *Why has there been no justice? No repercussions.*

If I'm being completely honest, I have to say that, as a mother of sons, it rarely crosses my mind that my children might someday become the victims of rape. Even though thousands of men are raped every year. What I do think about constantly is what would happen if they became victims of any kind of violence. A schoolyard bully beating them up behind the playground. A random stranger mugging them for their wallet or bus money when they're at the park. A drunk driver jumping a curb and hitting them with their vehicle.

These scenarios play in my mind on a constant loop every time I send them out into the world. And I know beyond a shadow of a doubt that I would burn down any civilization that would not grant justice to my children after they'd survived violence at the hands of another. So, when I opened up to my parents about the assault by way of telling them about *Flare* picking up my essay, I didn't feel any animosity in the face of their initial reactions. In fact, I was pleasantly surprised.

I'd had momentary thoughts about them being ashamed of me—not so much because I was raped, but because I'd been foolish enough to put myself in that position to begin with. My brain assumed that they would see our foray into a non-traditional marriage as the catalyst for my poor choices and, since there was no man with a mug shot to blame, they would turn that blame squarely on to me. But they didn't. They weren't ashamed at all, but they were angry—angry at the person who had hurt their child and angry that there was nothing, essentially, they could do about it. And I understood that.

Which made it all the sweeter when the essay finally came out late in the summer, and my email inbox, social media DMs, and Facebook timeline flooded with not only supportive messages from friends, family, and even students from the yoga studio, but also quiet thank-you's from other women—all over the world—who had experienced similar trauma and related to my story. When I could show my parents, Joe, and Kami that the article was making an impact. That it hadn't all been for nothing. I could see it lessen the amount of the pain they carried for me. And even though Farrah would continue to repeatedly remind me, at our now twice-a-month meetings, that I wasn't supposed to be playing caregiver during this time, I had to admit it felt good to know the emotional wringer I had put myself through in order to write about the assault was helping someone else.

And apparently would continue to do so—as more and more of the pitches I had sent out during the first few months after the retreat were starting to come back with recognition from the *Flare* piece and happy acceptance. Of course it wasn't like I could quit my job at the yoga studio. And the petite payments coming in for blog posts, podcast appearances, or interviews with badass female runners and cyclists weren't about to fund retirement for Joe and my parents. But it was forward motion, and even though every time I pitched another essay or article I held my breath, the process wasn't so scary anymore.

It felt like the world was starting to accept not only my story, but also the stories of thousands of other women, and that acceptance kept my nose to the keyboard on lunch breaks, after bath time, and late into the night. I'd found purpose and direction, and I felt a little unstoppable. Which, because the universe can be cruel sometimes, is exactly when the road ahead of me started to crumble.

* * *

One year and two days after my assault, on September 27, 2018, Dr. Christine Blasey Ford stood in front of the Senate Judiciary Committee of the United States—made up entirely of scowling, judgemental, old conservative men—and recounted the night that then Supreme Court Justice nominee Brett Kavanaugh "allegedly" sexually assaulted her during the summer of 1982, when they were teenagers.

Since early the previous fall, there had been wave after wave of public allegations against powerful men. Many were driven by the #MeToo movement. Begun by survivor and activist Tarana Burke, the social movement against sexual abuse, sexual harassment, and rape culture saw countless survivors publicizing their experiences of sexual violence or sexual harassment.

But this particular case had captured the attention of the world. In part, I think, because this time it wasn't just another powerful Hollywood player in the spotlight. This was a man potentially being elected into an incredibly influential position within the United

States government. A man who would be given the power to rule over that country and its governing laws, many of which were already in a terrifying backslide for women's basic human rights. It felt like every woman, everywhere, was holding one collective breath. The outcome of the hearing would either be a benchmark in history for sexual assault survivors, or a horrific snapshot of what was to come.

* * *

Other than for my scheduled appointments with Farrah, the odd dentist visit for the kids, or the very seldom holiday we took as a family, I rarely asked for time off work. It wasn't like my paycheque from the yoga studio was the one keeping us afloat, but I had been raised with an iron work ethic that often backfired and left me burnt out. So, when the Ford-Kavanaugh hearing was nearing its end and a decision was set to come down any day, I requested a few days, knowing full well either outcome was going to affect me.

Farrah had actually taught me this trick—pre-emptive sheltering, she called it. Essentially, if I knew an event, conversation, or interaction was approaching that might trigger some trauma memories or feelings, I would take action ahead of time to set myself up to process those feelings in a healthy way. That is, don't wait to practise self-care until you feel like your chest has been cracked open with anxiety and your only option is to inhale enough coke to make your problems disappear for eight to ten hours. Hence the use of a few days of my vacation time.

During that time off, I figured it wouldn't do me any good to just sit around the house worrying about the outcome, so I tried to channel my anxious energy into hitting the pavement. Since the retreat, I had slowly gotten myself back into running three or four days a week, usually after supper when the kids were settling in for the night, but occasionally—and only after a torturous few rounds of playing chicken with myself and my shadow—early in the morning before the sun had even risen.

Most people don't understand how I can enjoy running, let alone running that early, but it's my happy time. The world is still quiet with only the earliest of birds waking up and cheering me on with their twitters. Sometimes I get the timing just right and get to watch the sunrise paint the road with its warm orange and yellow hues. It feels like the newest part of every day. And returning to my early morning runs became yet another recovery milestone that I was determined to achieve.

The morning the Senate Judiciary Committee was set to vote on Kavanaugh's nomination, I did just that. I got out and pounded the pavement until my legs shook. But it wasn't enough, and after I dropped the kids off at school, I changed into a fresh running outfit, threw my water bottle and sneakers into the car, and headed to a nearby secluded trail I'd run once or twice when we'd first moved to Ontario.

When your feet hit soft dirt, even with its scattered tree roots and stones that have to be avoided, there's a different reverberation. Maybe it has to do with being surrounded by towering pine trees, or maybe it's the smell of freshly fallen leaves or broken soil. Either way, unlike hitting pavement, which slams your bones together in a sometimes jarring way, the impact of running on trails travels throughout your whole body. The vibrations awaken something that I think has been long dormant in humans. Something that wants to keep moving. Which was what I did until the buzzing in my armband distracted me so much that I almost went head over heels down a small slope.

Plucking one headphone from my ear I glanced over both shoulders. The trail was quiet today—save for the odd family with a golden retriever or the occasional older couple, hand in hand—but the habit of watching my own back still hadn't faded. Pulling my cell phone from the pouch on my arm band, I swiped across the screen to see it filled with new notifications. Without hesitation I clicked on the first one, CNN News, and read the headline as it popped up:

The Senate Judiciary Committee voted 11 to 10 in favour of Brett Kavanaugh's nomination to the Supreme Court.

Immediately, the air in my lungs hardened like cement. I flipped over to Twitter and scrolled frantically through the tweets.

There was celebration from the right-wing conservatives who felt justice had been served, but mostly, there was sheer devastation from women who saw this as yet further proof that sexual assault victims are guilty until proven innocent. And if the accused has enough money and enough power, their victims will always be the ones to blame.

I wanted to cry. My stomach lurched and threatened to bring back the contents of my breakfast. Fists clenching at my side, I had the sudden urge to hit something. There was this overwhelming feeling of anger and helplessness that, a few months ago, would have sent me searching for a dose of apathy. But this time I didn't want to give it away. I wanted to use it as fuel.

Tucking my phone back into my arm band along with my headphones, I struck out again on the path. This time much faster than I'd ever comfortably run before. Going slow no longer felt like an option. If I wasn't at a full-out sprint, what was the point? I concentrated on my rapid footfalls, trying to pay attention to the uneven ground below me so that I wouldn't eat shit and fall face first into the dirt. My quickened pace also helped me drown out the thoughts that had been stirred up. But I wasn't so consumed with concentration to not hear the second set of footsteps coming up behind me.

Glancing over my shoulder, I saw a man about 200 paces back—middle-aged, dark hair under a navy blue ball hat, a black and silver T-shirt with matching running shorts, tall and definitely fit enough to keep up with my pace. Rationally, I knew he was likely just another runner using the trail to get off the streets for a change. But my brain had given up reason when everything stopped making sense, and it was now focused solely on keeping me alive. No more, no less.

Thinking quickly, I veered off the main path and took a less travelled one that cut around a small pond. I quickened my pace, darting around a content elderly couple who stood at the edge of the water, tossing chunks of bread to the ducks. It would have been a lovely moment to take in if I hadn't been checking over my shoulder every thirty seconds to see if I'd lost the man.

As I rounded the west side of the pond, a frantic glance told me I had not. Now gaining with his long muscular legs, the man was close enough that I could hear every thud of his sneakers on the dirt. *Thud, thud, thud, thud.* The sound synced in my ears with the beating of my pulse and became deafening. In another quick move, I turned onto a gravel path more commonly used by bikers and circled back toward the parking lot. My route made literally no sense, and so it surely should have thrown off my follower. But to my dismay, when I looked over my shoulder before sprinting through the wooden gates of the parking lot, the man was not only still behind me but nearly overtaking me.

I skidded to a stop in the gravel, almost toppling over, and spun to face the stranger. A few months ago I would have continued my sprint, launching myself into the driver's seat of my car and slamming the locks into place. I was still afraid then. Now I was just pissed.

"What the fuck?" I screamed in his face. "Why the fuck are you following me!?" My fists were balled at my sides, my nails digging into the palms of my hands. The man looked down at me, his eyes wide and confused, which only made me more irate. "Women can't even go for a fucking run in the woods anymore without some piece of shit tailing them. Do you know what it's like to feel like fucking prey? Like you're being stalked every time you leave your house?"

He threw his hands up in the air and that's when I saw them. My keys, dangling from his fingers. Frantically, I patted my pockets and the arm band where I'd stashed them along with my phone.

"You dropped these a ways back." He held out his hand slowly and dropped them into mine. "Figured you might need them." They must have fallen from the pouch when I pulled my cell phone out in a rush to check the news notifications.

The wave of anger dissolved into utter embarrassment. "Oh wow, I am so sorry. I shouldn't have assumed..."

There were no words to finish that sentence because I *should* have assumed. I had no choice but to assume. What some people can never, and will never, understand is that the monsters who rape and murder women, they don't look like monsters. They don't have fangs or horns or scaly skin. They look like every other Joe Blow, which means it's up to us to decide whether he's "one of those guys" or not. And, as I now knew, if you made the wrong decision, you had to live with the consequences.

He nodded in acknowledgement of my apology and jogged back to the trail, where I'm sure he spent the rest of his run cursing his generous nature. I retreated to my car, picked up my phone, opened a new email tab, and started writing.

* * *

It was more or less the same story I'd been telling for a little while now—except this time, it was a brave young editor from a world-renowned publication who took a chance on it, and me. *Runner's World* magazine was a niche publication—part of the Condé Nast family that is legendary for publications like *Vogue* and *Harper's Bazaar*—but that didn't make it any less exciting to see that international number come up on the caller ID when they accepted the pitch I'd sent in a fury the day of the Kavanaugh confirmation vote. That acceptance also came with a significantly higher pay rate, wider audience reach (published in more than twelve countries), and a professional photographer to catch my early morning runs in action.

All in all, it felt like another milestone. And it explained how I came to be standing in the middle of the street in the early morning dark—illuminated only by a pool of light from the streetlight above me as snowflakes softly fell—trying my darnedest to smize for the camera. *Click. Click. Click.*

Allie, my editor for this piece about finding the courage to reclaim my early morning runs after being raped, was the one who had insisted the magazine spring for a photographer to come up from Toronto and take some shots. This was definitely a departure from the "send in a few selfies" protocol I'd gotten used to, and I was tremendously nervous. The only photographers I had worked with in the past had been men, and I wasn't quite sure a man would be able to capture the nuance of my story from behind the lens. That, and I was far from being a model.

Short, chubby, with a sometimes-crooked smile and no idea how to find my light, I was relieved when, well before sunrise, all five foot two of my photographer, Jennifer Roberts, knocked on my door. She was kind and quiet, quick to make me feel comfortable. Which I was thankful for as I stood in the street outside my house, her camera flash lighting up the snow and the faces of Joe and the boys peeking through the curtains of our front window, watching Mom trying desperately not to look foolish. They were still sleepy, but I could feel their pride through the frosted glass.

It almost made me dizzy, the rush of happiness, pride, and fear—the good kind. It felt foreign but familiar, like maybe I had known it once.

After I'd awkwardly run a few laps up and down the paths near my house, the sun started to break the horizon and we neared the end of the shoot.

While Jennifer sent her assistant to fetch another battery pack, she cleared her throat and spoke. "Did you know that usually the creative team doesn't read the pieces we work on? We get a sort of synopsis and mood guide, but that's generally it." I nodded, completely ignorant to the publishing process of magazines and unsure what she was getting at. "But Allie sent me your story to read before we shot, and I'm really glad I did." She fiddled with a dial on her camera. "What you're doing, telling your story, it's really brave."

I laughed nervously, the cold starting to chill the top of my nose. "I don't know about brave so much as self-serving." I blew on my hands to keep them warm. "I pitched this piece during a really tough time, and definitely wrote it as an act of catharsis."

She nodded, not in a patronizing way but in a way that said she understood, that maybe she'd been in a similar space at some point and knew how it felt to find any way to release.

"I'm sure it helped to get it all out, but trust me, this kind of thing will help a lot of other women too. Not everyone has your guts."

A thread of worry nipped at my earlobes along with the chilly winter wind. "Guts?"

Jennifer nodded again, a little more absentmindedly this time as she retrieved the battery pack from her assistant and hooked it to her light. "Sure, because when you dare to put your story out there, other people feel entitled to give you their opinions on it, whether you like them or not."

Other people's opinions had always been a concern of mine, but when the *Flare* essay came out to such a positive response—even though I wasn't naive enough to believe there weren't people out there smiling to my face and whispering behind my back—the idea of having to defend myself against naysayers had sort of faded into the background. But Jennifer's words had stirred up that old thread of worry. Now it sunk a little deeper into my bones even as I tried to brush it off as just another ghost of my trauma.

* * *

Over and over, I hit the refresh button on the computer screen, sneaking just a little self-indulgent time in between classes at the studio. There on the screen were my pink cheeks and bright green eyes set against the background of a dark street. The headline—"After a violent sexual assault, running gave me my life back"—was slightly more dramatic than the few I had suggested, but either way it was there, commanding attention on the main page of the *Runner's World* website. It had only been up for a few days, but Allie had emailed to let me know it was already clocking some of their best traffic for a personal piece. It all felt a little too good to be true.

"Have a great night, Sherry! Tell Jim we miss him in Hatha." I waved to the last of the night's clients and went about shutting down the rooms, mopping the floors, and tidying the bathrooms. I hummed to myself as I worked and barely even noticed Janine as she entered the locker room. She gently tapped me on the shoulder so as to not startle me, but I jumped nonetheless. Old habits.

"Oh my gosh, hey." I nervously laughed and clutched my chest. "I didn't realize you were still here. I thought everyone had left."

She softly ran her hand over my shoulder, the spot where she had tapped me. "I wanted to say congratulations before I headed out. I read your essay." Janine shook her head as she looked down at me, her blond hair damp from the warmth in the classroom. "Eden, you're a warrior. You know that, right?"

I did not, in fact, know that. But when Janine said it, with her earnest tone and kind eyes, I almost believed her. "Aw, Janine. Thank you. Coming from you, that means a whole lot." We both leaned in for an embrace, meeting in the middle and holding tight until it felt just right to release. Often, I still felt very solitary with people only in the peripheries of my life. Most likely because that's where I kept them, especially since the assault. I barely had the bandwidth to navigate my own care, let alone that of others. But moments like this, genuine moments of connection, made me think that opening myself up again might have been worth it.

Later that night, after locking up, I was again scrolling through my essay while sitting in the dark enclosure of my car before heading home. It felt a little like when the boys were still newborns and, even though I was exhausted, I couldn't put them down, couldn't stop marvelling at them. As I reread my words, flicking my finger over the screen and slowly scrolling to the bottom of the page, something I hadn't seen before caught my eye. The comment section.

None of my other pieces that had been published online had comments turned on. Sure, if someone wanted to seek out my Instagram or Facebook they could try to send me a message, but my privacy settings were pretty tight, and only the kindest of words had filtered through. But as I read these comments—an age-old mistake in this era of online media—I started to realize that some of them were very different from the praise I'd previously received.

Guest823770   18 December 2018

"Polyamorous" is one of those labels created by people who want to feel okay about their destructive behaviour so they spin things like—medical marijuana (drug use), or socially responsible pornography (human trafficking), etc... You poor girl—I hate what happened to you. Just know that whatever you're looking for in a swinger's lifestyle can be found legitimately, without endangering yourself or your family's well-being.

Guest636665   17 December 2018

I agree with you. Why get married if you're polygamous? No one deserves what happened to her but you have a kid at home... Why are you meeting random strangers alone for potential hookups? Totally irresponsible conduct.

These were probably the best of the worst. I would later find out that the awful, venomous ones had been quickly deleted by the page administrators, but these had somehow remained. A few kind commentors had tried to come to my defence, but the damage had already been done. These faceless strangers weren't just commenting on or criticizing my writing, my skill, the thing I was passionate about. They were cutting through who I was as a person, laying the blame for my assault squarely on my shoulders—the exact same way I had for months afterwards, and the same way I'd feared people would do if I opened up with my story.

There was nothing I could do to stop myself from internalizing their words. Like poison-tipped barbs, they stuck to my throat and seeped into my system, tainting all of the work I had done with Farrah, with Joe, on my own since the assault. I had come so far. And yet, with a few clicks of their keyboards, a handful of people I'd never known, and never would, had set back my climb from rock bottom who knows how far.

And as I sat there in the dark, fighting back tears, wishing I could reach through the screen in my hand and shake those people who had judged me, all I could think was:

What the fuck is the point?

CHAPTER 15

Returning
to the Scene

THE MONTHS THAT CAME AFTER MY *Runner's World* ESSAY WAS
released passed slowly, as if I was trudging through waist-deep
snow. That it was the dead of winter in Canada surely didn't help,
but neither did the rampant negative self-talk that played on a loop
in my mind. It felt like a familiar spiral, but instead of nosediving,
this time I simply became reclusive for a period of time. Pushing
back my appointments with Farrah, only half participating in the
holidays, accepting and then backtracking on writing assignments
I was in no place to be working on.

Even when I returned to my sessions with Farrah, I couldn't
shake the shadow of apathy that seemed to follow me everywhere,
casting everything in a muted hue.

"I know you've been having a hard time these last few months,
but I really think you need to give yourself more credit for how far
you've come in such a short time." Farrah reached across the table
and patted the back of my hand. She had taken to offering me more

physical affection lately. I wasn't sure if I had been giving off vibes of needing it or if she simply felt I was ready to accept it. "Very, very few people would be ready to share what they've gone through so soon after their assault. That took a lot of guts."

I scoffed. "There's that term again—guts. I don't think I had guts; I think I was grasping at straws. Didn't know what else to do to make something so fucking meaningless mean something."

"And you did," she squeezed my hand this time, almost as if she was begging me to be present. "Not only for yourself, but for a lot of other women. You saw it yourself with all those messages you received."

Pulling my hand away, I rubbed the skin where she had touched. "I also saw all the messages from people who said it was my fault and that if I wasn't such a slut, or I hadn't stepped outside my marriage, it would never have happened."

There was a heavy silence between us for moment. Then Farrah spoke, her voice calm but firm. "Do you honestly believe them?"

Without hesitating, I replied, "No." I rubbed the spot on my hand harder, the skin growing pink. "Doesn't mean it didn't make a dent."

Farrah plastered a smile on her face and nodded. "And dents can be buffed out." She read through her notes. "Last time you were here, you mentioned that you thought Joe might surprise you with something for Valentine's Day. Any idea what it might be?"

The corners of my mouth turned up slightly, thinking of the big cheesy red card Joe had presented me with the weekend before, a printed and detailed itinerary on the inside.

"Actually, I do. He must be taking lessons from you because he said he could tell I was in a rut and decided to force me out of it with a weekend away by myself in Montreal."

Farrah's excitement over this romantic gesture faded when she doubled back on the solo-trip part. "Alone? In a different city? Are you comfortable with that?"

Folding my hands in my lap, I consciously willed myself to stop rubbing my skin. "Well, I guess the original plan had him coming with me, but our babysitter fell through last minute and he already had everything booked." I shrugged. "I have family in Quebec, and have visited a number of times. Montreal is surprisingly one of the cities I feel the most comfortable in."

"It is a lovely city and the people are so sweet." She chuckled. "As long as you're not driving."

"I'll be cautious." We both nodded, knowing the deeper meaning of the sentiment.

"If you need anything while you're there"—Farrah scribbled on the back of a white business card—"text or call me. I'm really not supposed to do this, so burn this when you get home but I don't want you to feel like you're on your own while you're there."

I took the card and held it in my palm. It was a small gesture, the kind that had slowly filled in the cracks when I'd first come to her, broken and crumbling. I was thankful it seemed to still be working.

* * *

Joe had set me up in a sweet little hotel near Chinatown in the centre of Montreal. When I'd visited in the past, it had either been as a child to see my mother's sister and much older cousin, or on a field trip to the Biodome. Neither of which had allowed me to explore the parts of the city that weren't frequented with tourists. Thankfully, it being mid-February and a bitter cold winter, the streets were relatively empty except for the odd bachelor party group and locals.

On the first day away, I had expected to spend the majority of my time in the room ordering takeout and just generally wallowing under the grey cloud that seemed to follow me everywhere lately. But my hunger got the best of me after the six-hour drive and I decided to go for a wander to find something to fill my belly.

When I was younger, I had dreamed endlessly of travelling to faraway countries and immersing myself in cultures other than my own. It was one of the reasons I had loved my mother's collection of *National Geographic* magazines so much. Obviously becoming a parent had put a pause on any international roaming. It was also true that travelling—when it wasn't for work—wasn't Joe's cup of tea, but he always understood how strong my urge to explore was and always would be. So, as the kids got older and the odd dollar or two freed up, we had made a pact to never let a year go by without my seeing at least one new place. Even if it wasn't far. However, we had to do it.

There was the time I picked up a job from one of Joe's old business partners and spent a weekend driving a massive sprinter van from Halifax to Cape Breton, ferried to Channel-Port aux Basques, Newfoundland, and then completed an eleven-hour night drive across the island to St. John's. Or the time I impulsively bought a plane ticket during a seat sale and flew to New Orleans, where I stayed with a friend and we spent a week dancing through the streets during Mardi Gras, eating beignets, gumbo, and seared alligator.

Remembering these adventures as I wandered the streets of Chinatown—taking in the brightly painted archways, the smell of freshly cooked dumplings, the sound of street merchants haggling in a beautiful mix of Mandarin and broken French—revived that urge. That itch to see and experience and immerse myself in life outside the four walls of my home. It also reminded me of how brave I used to be.

Rarely did I ever travel with anyone, and I almost always went on a whim, figuring it out when my feet hit the ground. That kind of fearlessness felt expensive now. Like payment had come due for all my years of risk-taking when Liam pulled me into that car, and now I was back at zero. A few months prior, this might have been a sad thought. Hell, after reading those comments, it would have felt like a just sentencing. But zero wasn't the end—it was where it all starts. A place to grow from, a place to rebuild. My eyes were far more open now, and what I'd considered to be risks before felt like mere hiccups compared to what I'd recently survived.

Later in the day, after stocking up on a few trinkets to bring home to the boys and a tote bag full of second-hand books that smelled of dust and faded ink, I came across a little hole-in-the-wall art supply store. Avenue des Arts was just west of Parc du Mont-Royal and situated in the basement of a tidy row of stone buildings that appeared to have stood there since well before I was born. Anywhere I went, if I found a bookstore or a stationary shop and had even an inkling of suspicion that there might be new notebooks inside to add to my ever-growing pile (even though the majority of them sat pristine without a single page yet tarnished by ink), I could not resist venturing inside. And this little store called to me.

Climbing down the steps to the basement shop inside, I saw the original brick still lining the walls and tall, towering shelves in neat rows that funnelled the customers toward the back of the store. On the shelves were endless stacks of notebooks, a rainbow of acrylic, oil or watercolour paints, charcoal sticks, fine line markers, and boxes of clay. There was also a honeycomb stack of paper rolls and bins filled with canvases of all sizes. It was truly an artist's haven.

Toward the front of the shop, something other than notebooks caught my eye. A maze of glass-topped cases lined the checkout area. Nestled safely inside them was the most beautiful collection of pens I'd ever seen. As I was ogling these pens, the shopkeeper, a small, frizzy-haired older gentleman, appeared from behind the register and began describing each pen in great detail and rapid-fire French. Regrettably, and to the chagrin of my Acadian ancestors, my French was not (and still is not) the greatest.

I waved my hands to get the man's attention as he pulled a tray of brightly coloured pens from the case. "I'm so sorry. I don't speak good enough French." He tilted his head and stared at me, confused. Summoning the fraction of the language I could remember from Grade 8, I spoke slowly. "Anglais. Je ne parle bien Francais." I was sure my patronizing pace would infuriate him, but he simply chuckled and repeated himself in a clipped French-English hybrid.

"These are best pens you will ever hold. Look, look." He plucked a fountain pen from a tray and thrust it into my hand. "Feel. The weight is light, smooth tip, and ink is delicate." I couldn't deny it—it was a stunning pen—but when I took a look at one of the price tags, I immediately dropped it back into its velvet bed.

"Oh no, these are beautiful, but I think they are an investment meant for real writers."

Again, he cocked his head to the side and peered at me over his glasses, his dark blue eyes shaded by the silver wisps of his brows. "Do you write?"

I nodded, sheepishly.

"Then you are a writer."

With the swiftness and surehandedness of someone who had been passionate about pens his whole life, the shopkeeper retrieved a pad of paper from beside the register, selected a few pens—fountain, ballpoint, and felt—and proceeded to spend the next thirty minutes ignoring any other customer and enthralling me with his knowledge, from the history of ink wells to the density of writing paper and which tip was better for poems or prose.

By the end of his sermon, despite the protest of my bank account, I'd chosen a sleek black fountain pen with a silver tip and three cartridges of ink.

Handing me my receipt, the shopkeeper gazed at me like a proud father giving a child their first bicycle and said, "This is the pen you will write your novel with."

Having not mentioned to him that I wrote anything other than a few essays and a handful of unfinished fantasy books, I was a little taken aback.

"Oh no, I just write about my life experiences here and there. Definitely not something to write a book about. Plus, I don't know if I could even write a whole book."

He plucked the pen from my hand and carefully placed it in its box, gathered together a few extra pen tips and said, in a very matter-of-fact way, "You will."

I sensed this wasn't meant to be challenged, so I handed him cash, thanked him, and left with a pen I couldn't afford and an itch I hadn't scratched in a while.

* * *

The next day, filled with motivation from my trip to Avenue des Arts, I spent the day wandering through the museums and parks, eating delicious Portuguese food and reading on frosty park benches. And when the day started to wane, knowing it was my last night in Montreal, I found that I didn't want to order cheap takeout and eat in bed. In fact, I had a craving. Tequila and guacamole.

Slipping into a bar with brightly painted *calaveras* on the walls and cozy velvet chairs tucked into the corners, I pulled up a stool at the very end of the bar where I could lean my back against the short wall next to the front window and look out over the crowd. I ordered the nachos, fish tacos, and a fresh margarita with lime.

The smells from the kitchen wafted over the noisy chatter of the patrons and were nearly more intoxicating than the tequila. But what really caught my attention was the almost musical harmony of French, Spanish, and English twining together. There was also a steady thrum of drums and acoustic guitar playing through the speakers, meaning I only caught parts of the surrounding conversations, but even those fragments sparked a curiosity in me—one I remembered from my time at Pelee Island and, even before that, from a childhood spent watching the world interact around me and silently taking it all in.

Reaching into my bag, I pulled out one of the notebooks I had brought from home and fumbled for the pen I'd snagged from the hotel side table. Feeling the small box I'd picked up the day before brush against my fingers, I pulled out the fountain pen and marvelled as the low lights glinted off the silver tip. Maybe it was my belly filled with delicious food, or the tequila warming my throat. Or maybe it was the distance from my fears and shame that gave me a fresh perspective. Whatever it was, it guided my hand to the page and I started writing.

Two more drinks and a plate of warm olives, oil, and bread later, I looked up to see the bartender approaching. "Just letting you know we're doing last call soon, but absolutely no rush."

A sudden wave of anxiety washed over me, and I swivelled in my seat to look out the window. The dark of night had fallen over the city without my noticing. It was beautiful with the glowing lights of Montreal casting sort of a gothic glow. But it also meant I would have to walk back to my hotel, in the dark, alone. Before I could quell it, an old panic started to fill my chest.

"Ma'am?" I felt a gentle touch tap on my hand. Turning, I saw a small woman, dark brown dreads spun into a loose knot on the top of her head and a winged liner sharper than most of my kitchen knives.

"Sorry, I didn't realize how late it was." I fumbled for my phone, disappointed when the wait for an Uber was longer than the bar would be open. "Should have booked a cab earlier, apparently."

Her thick French accent tickled my ears as she chuckled and leaned on the bar. "Yeah, they don't bother coming downtown at this time of night. Get sick of taking tourists to the airport hotels. Are you staying close by or far out?"

I tucked my phone away. "No, no. I'm just a few blocks over by Chinatown. I can walk it."

She pressed her palm to the back of my hand, her long nails running across my skin and leaving a trail of goosebumps. Without hesitation she said, "No. I'll walk with you."

Before I could thank her but politely decline, she'd whispered something to the other bartender and grabbed her tips and jacket. She waved for me to follow her as she headed toward the door, lighting a cigarette before slipping on bright pink knitted mittens. I hurried to catch up, shrugging into my jacket and stuffing my notebook and pen into my bag.

"Are you sure? If it's out of your way, seriously I can make it on my own. It's not that far."

She slowed slightly and linked her arm through mine, which was when I realized she was nearly a head shorter than me. Blowing a puff of smoke in the opposite direction, she looked up at me, her smile bright against the depth of her skin. "None of us make it on our own. If we don't look out for each other, who will? Right? Right."

She nodded in answer to her own question and continued to chatter on about her evening at the bar while we walked the two blocks to my hotel. All the while, my head swam. Maybe a little from the margaritas, but mostly from the very small, likely inconsequential act this sprite-like human had just done for me. It occurred to me that she would never truly understand its impact.

I knew I wouldn't be able to pay her back, so to speak, but the words she'd spoken continued to resonate with me long after my weekend in Montreal.

If we don't look out for each other, who will?

* * *

When I returned from my weekend away, I was almost instantly swept back up into the everyday rush of parenting and—with a promotion at the studio to a more managerial position, more hours and more responsibility—the creative muse I had picked up in the city reluctantly took a back seat.

Months went by and winter faded to summer, time seeming to pass so much quicker now that I wasn't just watching the world from my prison of trauma. Don't get me wrong; I wasn't cured. There is no cure for that kind of damage to the soul. My heart still tried to jump out of my chest when a loud noise surprised me. The smell of certain colognes still made my skin crawl. And, occasionally, a hand on my neck still made me cower. I'd learned that there was no road map to recovery, but as long as you were moving forward, it was progress nonetheless.

With summer came our annual pilgrimage back to the East Coast. Due to a mix-up with Joe's work schedule the summer before, this would be our first time back since the assault—and, in turn, the first time I'd see my family face to face since I'd been open with them about what I'd gone through. I was afraid—there was no denying it—but not of their judgment. I was afraid things would be different.

Occasionally, I still felt the people around me treating me a little like a bird with a broken wing. Too tender and precious. My family had never been that way. Which was likely why I had developed such a thick skin. I knew now that this wasn't always the healthiest solution to life's challenges, but in my eyes, it was better than being pitied or tiptoed around.

* * *

As on most of our trips back home, we set up residence at a campground not far from our parents. This way, the kids could get an outdoor adventure experience as well as family time. A few days into our vacation, I found myself sitting on the back steps of my father's house, just thirty minutes outside of Halifax.

The houses were a little farther apart out this way, and the smell of the ocean was faint in the air. I watched the boys as they ran and played in the yard with their cousins—my niece and nephew. Every time I noticed how much they had grown, I wished for more time and less distance, but I knew in my heart we were all where we were meant to be.

"Remember when they were just babies? Seriously, how are they so big?" Kami took a long drag off her cigarette as she leaned against the deck railing, watching the kids.

"They're certainly growing up fast, but"—I pointed to the gaggle of arms and legs as the kids rolled around giggling, without a single care in the world—"they're milking their childhood as long as possible, so we must have done something right."

Kami nodded. "All we can do is try."

I bobbed my head in unison. "Try to raise good men."

"And a strong woman." She smiled at my niece, who had just tackled one of the boys to the ground in a mock wrestling match.

"Oh, you won't have any issue with that; she's just like her aunt." I looked back to see that my mother had joined us. She was smiling, thinking she'd paid me a kind compliment. Then she added, "She'll scare all the boys away with that attitude."

"Mom, don't say that to her. The women in her life should be sticking up for her, not putting her down," I snapped, my tone likely sharper than it should have been. Turning away from Kami and Mom, I watched my niece run ahead of the boys in their impromptu footrace. "Any boy that thinks it's attitude and not spirit doesn't deserve her attention anyway."

I couldn't help but let my face fall. I'd thought we'd come so far, but this destructive ideology was still being inflicted on the younger generations. If you're too quiet, you're anti-social, maybe even a bitch. If you're too loud, you've got attitude and are asking for a fight. There's no right way to be a woman, apparently, other than to be obedient.

My mother waved her hand dismissively and snuck a pull from Kami's smoke. "Since when are you so sensitive?"

"I've always been—you just didn't notice because you were always busy with something else."

I didn't look back, but I could feel an old familiar tension settle in around us. Mom gave an exaggerated huff and retreated inside, followed by my sister. I inhaled deeply through my nose and out through my mouth, the way Farrah had taught me to after I'd confided that I would be heading home for a visit. I worked to push out all the frustration and pull in understanding. It was a lot harder in reality than it sounded in those aesthetically pleasing yoga videos or a therapy session.

As I rose from the steps, my father came out and gave a hoot to the grandkids that dinner was ready. I knew he'd likely heard the thorny conversation between me and Mom, and I was ready with an arsenal of snarky comments that would distract from my disappointment. But before I could open my mouth, he pulled me into a hug. The kind of hug he only gave out on birthdays, or when he gave me away at my wedding, or the day I left for Ontario.

It was an unexpected show of affection that left me wondering: If the chaotic energy of my mother and sister's overt emotions was sometimes more than my nervous system could handle, maybe the distant, stone-faced approach to relationships that I'd learned from my father wasn't the right way to go about things either.

Giving me one last squeeze with his massive arms, he whispered in my ear. "Don't take what she says personal. We all see things from different perspectives, and when things are different from the ones we know, it takes some time to get used to them."

He was right. If I wanted patience for my healing, then I should extend the same to hers.

After dinner, when the kids were snuggled together in front of the TV with Kami and Dad watching a movie, and Joe was helping himself to a second round of pumpkin pie, Mom called me into her bedroom. Immediately, I felt like a child, a heavy gut filled with guilt over who knows what infraction. *Was I too noisy while she was trying to nap? Did I lie for Kami again without knowing?*

"What's up?" I asked, as nonchalantly as possible. Coming through her door, I was surprised to find her sitting on the edge of her bed, tears streaming down her cheeks.

"Eden, I'm sorry."

"Sorry? For what? What happened?" I could feel a rush of panic. Even after the months of work I had done with Farrah, there was still this instinct to care for her, to never let her suffer.

"I'm sorry that I left you alone. So alone as a child that you couldn't even tell me when something so awful happened to you. That you felt more comfortable sharing it with the world than with your own mother," she sobbed into her hands.

"Oh, Mom, it's not that I couldn't tell you." I sat beside her on the bed and wrapped my arms around her shoulders. I tried to find the right words; this wasn't the conversation I had been expecting, and I certainly hadn't been expecting an apology for the abandonment I'd felt since I was little.

"I was never there for you, not when you needed me. Oh, Eden, I'm so sorry," she cried again, sniffing loudly.

"Mom, I know it wasn't easy for you. Even with Dad around as much as he was, you were still a single mom, trying to raise two"—I choked back a laugh—"spirited daughters. One of which was hell bent on destruction, and the other a fortress of solitude." My attempt at levity must have worked because I could hear her sobs slowing.

A year ago, I would have continued to smooth things over, to say whatever I had to keep the peace, but I needed more than just a few words of apology. I had been waiting nearly thirty years to say my piece, and I knew if I didn't seize the moment now I'd never be able to work on the part of me that still felt abandoned. "But you are right—you did leave me alone. For a very long time I fended for myself. Felt invisible. And when I did get a voice, it felt like all it did was annoy you."

She chuckled. "You had so many goddamn opinions."

We both laughed a little. "Who do you think I got that from?"

"Your father, of course."

The little dig pushed me on. "Either way, I do think that time in my life where I was either by myself or on the sidelines contributed to my inability to put myself before anyone else. Because why would I? I never felt like a priority in anyone else's life, so why would I be in my own?"

"Oh, Eden, I'm so sorry. I never intended to make you feel that way or to ever think you weren't a priority. Truthfully, when you were little, my only priority was just making it through the day. I didn't know it then but I was deeply depressed with no support for it and no real idea what to do." There was a quiet pause. "Regardless, I can't change the past, but I can tell you how sorry I am and that I'm going to try to make it up to you every day from now on."

I let out a breath—one I hadn't realized had been stuck in my chest for who knows how long. "Honestly, this is more than I could have hoped for. Thank you."

Hearing the rise of little voices coming from the living room, she wiped the wetness from her cheeks and smiled. "We would all be lucky if my granddaughter and your niece inherits even a little bit of that spirit from her aunt."

I leaned in and hugged her. The kind reserved for birthdays and departures. "Well, if it's any consolation, I think she inherited her annoyingly big heart from you." She playfully swatted at me and we made our way back to the group.

I knew in that moment that I could have torn into her, rehashed everything she'd ever said or done during my youth that had made me this way, that had made it so hard to undo the years of toxic caretaking or self-deprecation, but there was no point. I couldn't go back in time and change things. Just like I couldn't change my decision to open my marriage to Joe, or accept Liam's invitation to that date. And if I ever found the courage to go to the police and report what he had done to me, even that wouldn't allow me to hit rewind and stop that monster from violating me.

All we had was the choice to move forward or stay stuck, and I was tired of being stuck.

* * *

The rest of our trip went by in a flurry of family visits, date nights in Halifax at The Lower Deck pub, trips to the ocean, and more good food and good conversation than I'd had in a very long time.

Fussing with the French press as I brewed a fresh batch of coffee on our last morning, I was pleasantly surprised that I didn't flinch or jump when Joe came up behind me, wrapped his arms around my waist, and nuzzled in my neck.

"I can't believe we've been married ten years today," I whispered into the side of his cheek.

He grinned, his grown-out beard tickling my ear. "I can't believe you've put up with me for that long."

Elbowing him playfully in the side, I poured him a cup. "Well, now that you're making big bucks as a business owner and only shagging the side chicks I know about, it's so much easier."

This time he full-out laughed. "Life is a lot easier now that we can actually afford to feed our family, huh?" Peeking around and giving me a wink, he continued, "And now that I'm behaving myself."

"Easier, for sure. But it also feels like we're finally living our lives, you know? When we were here, it was great. We had our family and friends and the water." I pointed at the waves on lake just beyond the trees. "But for me, at least, it always felt like this limbo between being kids and growing up."

"Like we were stuck," Joe added.

"Exactly." I paused for a moment as Joe let me go to pour milk and a spoonful of sugar into his coffee. "Do you regret any of it? These ten years?"

Without even looking up he shook his head. "None of it. It wasn't all perfect, but it got us here." He nodded to the three boys still asleep inside the tent. "And here is pretty great."

After we finished our coffee, Joe insisted I get one last short run in before we hit the road. My practice had been off and on since the winter. Partially due to time and motivation, and partially due to emotional distraction. But knowing I'd be spending the next twenty-two hours in a hot, stuffy car with three vacation-wiped children, I took the opportunity to soak up as much of the East Coast as I could in the time I had left.

Setting out, I found a well-trodden trail and followed it over softly cresting hills, through dense pockets of evergreens and musky pine bedding. The trail snaked through the park and ambled back around the perimeter of the lake. When I made the circuit to head back toward our campsite, I noticed a fork in the path. One path led toward a cliff edge that I recognized from many lifetimes ago.

This park wasn't just the place we'd come every summer to camp; it was also legendary in my high school years for cliff jumping. The senior students would all take turns launching themselves off the rockface into the water below as a sort of testament to their youth. Or because of too much booze. Back in high school, I had never been brave enough to jump. And that hadn't changed during the summers we'd returned, when Joe, Declyn, and Cash would jump the sixty feet to the water without hesitation. I turned onto the footpath and started toward the edge.

Finding my way through the brush, I crept slowly until I could feel the wind on my face, no longer sheltered by the trees, and see the waves below me. It was still a long way down, but it had seemed so much farther before. And now that I was standing there, with everything that I'd experienced behind me, I couldn't understand what had been so scary.

Peeling off my sneakers, socks, and T-shirt, leaving me in only a sports bra and shorts, I tucked my cell phone into my shoes and inched closer to the edge. I had thought that everything after the assault would be the worst thing imaginable, like a never-ending marathon of pain and fear, but now I realized that if I could survive that, what the fuck else could stop me? Inhaling deeply, I closed my eyes and counted. *One, two, three.* I jumped.

The air rushed past my ears in a matter of seconds and then the water swallowed me up. The icy cold stopped my heart for a beat, and when I broke through the surface, I gasped at the humid summer air. I felt reborn. Swimming to the rocky shore, I pulled myself up onto a flat spot and looked out at the sun rising over the water. This was what living life—not just existing or surviving—was supposed to feel like. Sometimes there would be moments where I was forced back into survival mode, but that was okay, because all I had to do to get back to living was take the leap.

* * *

"Oh, I'm so happy to hear you had that epiphany!" Farrah clapped her hands together in such delight it made me laugh. I had just finished relaying to her the realizations I'd had with my family and myself on our trip back home.

I chuckled. "So now we're done, right?"

She tilted her head and smirked. "If only it were that easy. I will say, you have come a long way, and the work we do moving forward will only strengthen that resolve you've finally found."

"What's next then?" I folded my hands on the table and leaned in, almost excited for the coming challenge.

"You get to decide that. You've talked before about wanting to write more about your story. Have you considered expanding it into something like a collection of essays, or maybe a book?"

I thought back to the hateful comments some of my writing had received, but also to the beautiful messages.

"I have. I guess I just don't know where to start."

Farrah thought for a moment and then spoke. "Why not go back to where it started?"

I felt my pulse begin to quicken, but just a little. "The parking lot?"

She nodded. "Only if you think you're ready to face it. It could easily bring back memories you haven't tackled yet. But if you think you're strong enough, it could also give you the direction you have been searching for."

The idea of returning to the place where it all happened felt a little like walking into a lion's den. Would I just be asking to be thrust back into that trauma all over again if I did? Or was this the final test, the sort of grand finale, facing the big boss at the end of the game? Maybe it was time.

A few weeks later, just three days shy of the two-year mark, I pulled into the dusty parking lot where the assault happened. I parked, then hesitated for just a moment before getting out. I'd been expecting to be steamrolled with horrific mental images and pummelled with fear. Instead, I couldn't help but marvel at how different it looked during the day. The shadows were gone, and along with them, the monsters they had hidden. It was just a normal space, benign even.

After finally extracting myself from the car, I sat on the curb and placed my bag at my feet. Reaching inside, I pulled out a notebook. The same one that had come with me to Pelee Island and then Montreal. I was in a different destination now, but one that was just as foreign. I opened the notebook, waiting for that muse to speak up again. Nothing.

Flipping to the front, I found the spot where I'd attempted and failed, many times, to record what had happened that night in far greater detail than my essays had allowed. I noticed how my handwriting had changed from a frantic, scratchy scrawl to winding loops with more pause and prose. It reminded me of my recovery. How it had never been linear, but almost like being caught in the undertow of a wave.

Sometimes you could push yourself toward the surface for a gulp of air only to be pulled back under and thrown against the ocean floor, where the sand slipped through your fumbling fingers. Eventually, though, if you held your breath long enough, if you kicked and pumped your arms strong enough, you would find your way back to the shore. Half drowned and exhausted, but alive.

I flipped through the notebook, searching for a blank spot, when a torn piece of paper fluttered from between the pages to the ground. Picking it up, I squinted to read the slanted scrawl of the unmistakable handwriting of Margaret Atwood.

You have the story.

After the retreat, I had torn the small notation from my manuscript and tucked it into my notebook. It had been a souvenir stolen and cherished from our meeting. Now it was a ghostly reminder of a much greater purpose.

Tucking the scrap of paper back into my book, I began writing. Not a light-hearted fable about the consequences of dishonesty, but a call to action. One that would speak for all those who had been preyed upon by monsters and had their stories dismissed as nothing more than crying wolf. I decided my story would no longer be written just to save myself from the fatality of shame. Instead, I hoped for it to herald a new era for survivors. The ones who weren't blessed with closure or conviction. Who found themselves lost in a purgatory of fear and re-victimization. An era in which more of us could come forward, without trepidation that our innocence would be put on trial.

* * *

We were raised to be sheep. I refuse this narrative. In fact, I am writing my own. This time, I don't give a fuck about whether or not the townspeople would believe my cries; they've never come to my rescue and likely never will. I will no longer be just a part of the flock. I am the shepherd, taking my turn, watching for the wolf.

THE END

Acknowledgements

I NEVER WANTED TO WRITE THIS BOOK. I NEEDED TO WRITE THIS book.

In the beginning, writing this memoir was a purely selfish endeavor. I was drowning with absolutely no direction or purpose or anchorage in the midst of my recovery, and writing—something I had regularly used as an escape in my childhood—saved me. The pages of notebooks became the only places I felt safe to be truly honest about the war being waged in my mind. But eventually, with the encouragement of people I will thank here, I realized that this wasn't just my story. It belonged to many, many others, and if I was able to, it was my responsibility to speak for them as well.

Without the team at Book*hug, especially Hazel Millar, who took a chance on an unknown writer when I randomly slid into her direct messages, I'm not sure if this book would ever have made its way to you, the reader. Jay and Hazel, along with my editor Linda

Pruessen, have believed in me and my story even when I didn't, and for that, I am forever grateful.

Chelene Knight: When we first met as mentor and mentee, I would never have known how integral you would become to breathing life into this book. You have always championed it and my writing, and I will never know how to thank you enough for that. You are a goddess.

To the small circle of friends and family who have been cheering me all the way to the finish line, thank you. My fellow writers of the Pelee Island writing retreat, Rosemary and Jenn, thank you. Margaret, what can I say except for *fuck it* and thank you. Most notably, Kelly S. Thompson. You came into my life when I was already neck deep into writing this book, but if it hadn't been for your unwavering support, love, and encouragement, I might have crumbled under the weight of the emotional labour it took to finish it. Thank you.

Thank you to my father, an unshakeable oak tree of a man who taught me to swing a hammer, change a tire, and to be fiercely independent because, and I quote, "You should never *need* a man." To my mother, thank you for fucking up sometimes. It taught me that we are all human—even if I thought you were an otherworldly fairy person for a good portion of my childhood—and that the monsters in our heads are powerful, but not more powerful than the love we have for each other. My sister, Kami, thank you for letting me share some of your story and how it formed the indestructible bond we have today. There may have been times I've wished we could have had a more traditional little sister-big sister relationship, but I will never regret being your pittie.

To my sons, Declyn, Cassius, and Milo, thank you for not complaining when I had to work late into the evenings and on weekends, missing bonfires and movie marathons and bedtimes. Thank you for being proud of me, even if you still think I'm the least cool person on earth. And thank you for being the men the world needs now. You make me so happy to be your mother.

A special thanks to Joe. My best friend. You never wavered in supporting my writing this book and pursuing a lifelong dream of being an author. Even when the fridge was nearly empty and the bank account was running dry, you just worked harder and longer to keep the lights on. But not only that, you were the one who kept me from falling into a million pieces after my assault. You loved me even when I was broken, maybe even more fiercely. You believed me, and I can't thank you enough for that.

And to my very first believer, Bruce Watling, my uncle. It has been almost six years since you've left us, but every day that I have worked on this book I have replayed some of your last words to me in my head. *"If it doesn't satisfy your passion, don't do it."* You taught me to lean into my creativity and never devalue it just because it didn't pay the bills. You taught me to never settle for any less than exactly what I deserve. And your passing, ironically, taught me to live every single day as if there is no time left because one day there won't be. Thank you for leaving your mark on me and for encouraging me to leave my mark on the world. I wish you were here to see this.

Eden Boudreau was born and raised in a small rural area just out-side Halifax. In 2016, she relocated to Ontario with her husband and three sons. As a bisexual, polyamorous woman who has survived her fair share of adversity, Eden's work draws on her life experien-ces to inspire vulnerable and relatable stories. Her essays have been featured in *Flare*, *Today's Parent*, and *Runner's World*, among others. She is the host and creator of *The Lonely Writer* podcast, aimed at destigmatizing mental health struggles during the writing process. Boudreau lives in Georgina, Ontario. *Crying Wolf* is her first book.

Manufactured as the first edition of
Crying Wolf: A Memoir
In the spring of 2023 by Book*hug Press
Edited for the press by Linda Pruessen
Copy edited by Jo Ramsay
Proofread by Charlene Chow
Type + design by Michel Vrana
Printed in Canada
bookhugpress.ca